God's Work
in My Life

Doug Anderson

ISBN 979-8-89428-973-1 (paperback)
ISBN 979-8-89428-990-8 (digital)

Christian Faith Publishing
832 Park Avenue
Meadville, PA 16335
www.christianfaithpublishing.com

Printed in the United States of America

Churches from the Start

We went to a Swedish Church on Jackson Street in Joliet, Illinois. There was quite a bit of poverty and a time of negative racial treatment. My family early on was my two older brothers and Mom and Dad, of course. Morning and evening services were every Sunday and a Wednesday meeting for adults and children to learn more about Jesus. Our drive from Lockport to Joliet was driven by the old large limestone blocks, and we went by at least three times there and back. It held some of the most dangerous prisoners in Illinois. It was also the famous prison used in the *Blue Brothers* movie.

There was a Jewel store across from the church, and many of us kids would sneak across after Sunday school to get some candy sometimes before the main service. There also was a bar that we would walk by Dahlen's Paint Store, and JB and I, during dark nights, would sneak up to the main window, bang on the window, and take off running down the alley that led us back to church. This was after the service when parents were talking and talking. Never did get caught. Next-door drinkers were probably too drunk to catch us.

There was a two-story house next to the store of the church that was initially the home for a pastor and family. Like the church, it was very old even in 1960 when I started Sunday school. However, we used the upper parts of the house for us youngins, and we would come running to the house, rushing up the steep steps, that we were supposed to walk upon, and sit down to start singing songs. The first song was always "nine forty-five, nine forty-five, everybody to Sunday school at nine forty-five," and repeated a few times. Many other songs would also be sung like "Jesus Loves Me," "Jesus Loves the Little Children," "I've Got the Joy, Joy, Joy, Joy Down in My Heart," and "The B-I-B-L-E."

1

It was fun for me as I liked Jesus, and I liked to sing! There was a huge older lady by the name of Mrs. Dupere who walked slowly, and though she was large, she was very nice in the way she worked with us and taught us. After singing with some hand movements, we chilled out to listen to the Bible story and sometimes handcrafts. Then we would be watched *slowly* down the steep steps and be shoveled into our Swedish Baptist Church.

Inside the dark small brick steeple building, I would often go downstairs to take a pee. There was a little, very old man, slow cane-walking Mr. Dahlen, the owner of the paint store. He was short, about 5'5", and had thick glasses and squinting eyes with a big smile. For whatever reason, he used to be down there in the basement area, and he would come out of the bathroom, hopefully after washing his hands, and would hand out candy to kids. It was a hard ruby-colored piece called Red Anise Squares. It had a unique flavored taste, and JB and I would pray that he washed his hands before we suck on the hard candy.

After going upstairs across the large entry doors, we had wide steep steps again to walk up to enter the chapel and try to find our parents and brothers sometimes to sit next to them. My older brothers would often go up to the balcony seats and sit with their friends and/or girlfriends but participate in the service. Ingie would always be playing along with Lorraine Ackley, and Mom would usually be on piano and Lorraine on organ, but they switched every once and a while. They were both *super* players. My mom has been able to play the piano without needing sheet music of notes and, at the age of ninety-five, was able to sing the hymns! Wasn't she amazing? We often had Neil Swanson play his hot trumpet, my dad on his clarinet, David Berglund (JB's older bro) and his trombone, and many other quality Swedish musicians. Howie played a darn good sax too!

When I was still very young and occasionally could sit on the balcony with a brother, there were scary-looking closed little doors. I always wondered what was in them. When I was a couple of years older, I had a dream. In the dream, I was alone in the church, and it wasn't lit well. I turned around and looked up to the balcony, and I saw a large tiger who looked at me. The tiger disappeared until I saw

2

him taking his time to keep walking toward me by jumping down. I shouted out to him, yelling, "In the name of Jesus, get thee behind me!" Again, yelling, "In the name of Jesus, get thee behind me!" The tiger disappeared, and I woke, hopeful and thankful for the ending.

JB and I would often sit together when we grew up a bit. Our parents got together often, so JB and I would do our thing. In church, Jeff often liked to goof around. I remember him having a pin and sticking me off guard, and I yelled a quick surprised yell during a sermon, and my face turned red as an Anderson apple and my face down, giving JB a steady mean stare. He would also, on purpose, find some couple of old blue-haired ladies to sit behind. He liked to tickle a lady's fox fur around her neck. He also could use a strange way of opening his mouth, and a very light spray of spit would lightly fall on the hair of each lady. Right from his mouth and straight on their hair. They would be looking left and right and up and behind without knowing anything. If you are close to JB, you can expect he will be a part of it at the least.

I was baptized in this church. Grandpa Sam was the head deacon for a long time, and before I went under the water, I had to explain to all the deacons at once just why I wanted to be baptized. Grandpa helped me understand how important to pick and use the Scripture, believe it, and have faith in Jesus. He discussed with me what Scriptures meant the most to him, and at that moment, I chose my two verses on my own. I was prepared and very nervous to share my need to accept Jesus as my Savior. "For the wages of sin is death, but the gift of God is eternal life in Christ Jesus our Lord" (Romans 6:23). My other verse was "But God shows his love for us in that while we were still sinners, Christ died for us" (Romans 5:8). I have always loved Romans, especially in taking a hard but beautiful class at Moody Bible Institute, which came much later in life.

Pastor Merrit and his two sons brought many of the young guys to the boundary waters in northern Minnesota. JB was not able to come as his mom wouldn't allow him to go mainly because his older sister, Lynn, recently passed away after a long time of struggling physically but always staying close to Christ. Mom Gloria just didn't want him taking any chances, and that was a problem with him.

3

I did have John and Bobby Merrit as well as Steve Sandbloom to hang out with, fish, canoe, and get to know each other better. We collected dehydrated foods for most of the week and one fresh steak food for our first supper in the boundary. We were given our safety sermon, life jackets, ropes, small tents, multiple canoes, and paddles before we decided who would canoe with whom.

Once we took off, it was a beautiful day and calm waters. We had to carry our canoes and all of our gear to get from one section of the water to the next. At one time, we were caught in the middle of a large lake when the wind started blowing hard and white caps began quickly as we were getting splashed hard. We had groups of canoes connected by ropes so we wouldn't lose anyone (one of the sermon rules). With being joined together, we safely made it to an island where we set up for the day and night as things became calm as quickly as they became rough.

It was a blast as the sun came back out, and we set up camp and jumped in the cool water. Pastor Merrit caught a large northern and took it right away to get it weighed. There are no motors allowed anywhere in the huge boundary waters outside of Minnesota and Canada, so by the time Pastor got to weighing his northern, he lost some pounds. Still, it ended up being a twenty-four-pound northern!

Meanwhile, a couple of us guys, including Steve who was my tent partner, were throwing stones at the flying squirrels. Real nice, right? When we thought we hit one and we slowly snuck up on him/her, he/she would jump up and fly across to another tree. They were cool, controlled stinkers. A few of us went to the shore and started to do some fishing, I caught a nice walleye, and Steve and Bobby both caught largemouth bass. This is what we added to the supper that night, and we were very proud. I obviously have never forgotten the Merrit family and that they all loved the sports I loved and singing and helping others out if needed.

Pastor Merrit was originally from the Pittsburgh area and was a superfan of the Pirates and the Steelers. He also had kids at our church who would often get other kids to play basketball in the gym. I loved that—with the tall and older John Merrit and younger

Bobby, who both were strong players—we once all got together to play another church and kicked their butts (in the name of Jesus).

John ended up being pastor to a megachurch in California and Bobby preaching at a megachurch in Cambridge, Minnesota. Karen and I went to Bobby's church one Sunday just to hear him preach and have a little talk about the past and time in Joliet. I was glad to see him again. Sister Kathy who was my own age is the wife of a pastor who led at the Cook, Minnesota, Baptist Church. Small world! Our whole family got to see and hear them for at least one, if not two years, up north. I'm not sure where they went next; they might have been missionaries. Debbie was an old friend of my sister, Lori, and Jan was the youngest sister.

Dellwood Park

On the Fourth of July, every summer, our church would spend a long day at Dellwood. Big barrels of hot bubbling water would be working nonstop with the corn on the cob over and over. I love fresh corn! Most of the families would bring all kinds of things, especially food! Jell-O with fruits in it, green bean casseroles, cheesy dishes with scalloped potatoes, multiple dishes of different types of potato salad, homemade bread, biscuits, and much more! Some would work with the burgers and hot dogs and some with the Polish sausage and more so the Swedish sausage. Yum!

There would be running races with children, which I always won every year in my age group, and little prizes for all involved. Eggs being tossed from being close to getting further and further away until one set of partners would survive. Same thing with the water balloons when most kids just enjoyed getting splashed as did the parents, or did they? The cool water was welcomed on a hot summer day. Then the race with a partner where each person put a foot in a pillowcase to see which two could get to the finish line first.

Of course, there was ice cream, mucho pies, cakes, and cookies on multiple tables as well as cold pop and cold water from the close by water pump. Swings and a spin around were filled with happy laughing, smiling children while junior high kids would go down to the dam and the caves, which were a bit dangerous to go into, but teens do what they want to do. Those caves were eventually closed.

For me, it was always the most fun to watch the older teens play against the parents in softball. My dad Howie would play, and it was a blast to watch him rip a hard-hit ball and run pretty fast around the bases. He could do more than play great music! Of course, when my

6

brother Barry and Jim Peterson, and a few more hotshot teens started hitting the ball, it often went way out there. It makes me think of how my mom never saw me play any sport ever. She only saw Barry wrestling once and said she would never watch it again because she didn't want him hurt. She did go to one football game at Barry's senior last game homecoming with Bethel versus Hamline. It was a game where Barry got bumped as a defender, and he turned around to rip the turd right back!

Other Coming Churches

Pastor Price was the pastor of Rochester Community Baptist Church and also served on the school board. That is where I met him after going to him for a master class, and I totally loved the guy. We loved becoming a part of this church family. Many of the members were from Mississippi and Georgia. It was solid worship, and one of my favorite, if not all-time favorite, pastors I ever had. We also were able to help with a small church outside of Rochester, Minnesota. This then became a sad day when I was promised a deal with teaching at the same school after getting my master's in education, but the principal retired, and the new principal hired someone else even though I was promised to keep my spot, but other openings were not open either.

I would really miss baptisms in the lake with Pastor, singing in the choir, and eating giant delicious food that I wasn't familiar with but came to love. Things like like peach cobbler and ice cream, home-cooked jams, jellies, fried chicken, buttermilk pie, collard greens, and more. God bless all from that church!

Zion Baptist Minneapolis, Minnesota

For years, I asked any parents and their child or children if they would go to Zion Baptist Church to get a feel for a church of 97 percent black worshipers, and we could stop for lunch afterward if they wanted. It is a unique service that was preaching from the same Bible as other churches but just a different atmosphere. We had a few sets of parents come and appreciate the experience. That is when we went back to Eden Prairie for a job and looked for a good "black Baptist church." Karen and I joined the church choir singing with movement! Everyone would sing for much more than a half hour, followed by strong services and long prayers usually at the end.

I wrote a short "Last Supper" play for men to act out and also worked in Sunday school. Also, we had a day with my sister and family, the McCoys, and young Kate sang a song that Sunday and blew them all away. The church was rockin', and we were totally rockin' with our young niece too. My girls eventually had the experience of being a part of it too.

My Spiritual Destructions

Starting in church, family, and many sports,
Led into beer in junior high, first dope in eighth grade.
Into everything as a freshman, into partying as a priority.
By nineteen, an alcoholic began to grow.
Ten years went by, I was high on something almost every day.
Realizing I "was not doing what I wanted,"
But had no/little power over my own lusts.
Could put this in the very beginning from destruction to salvation.

8

Unaware of Satan/deceiver's damaging warfare.
Felt like a frog in boiling water.
Damage being done spiritually, physically, and mentally.
Cocaine and Marijuana took my life away.
A slow death was in process, destroying any power.
No self-esteem. My only hope was in my Jesus.
I clung to that through ten years of prayers and tears.
I was not fully delivered from my sinfulness.

Fearful, "He gave me over."
But I had many prayers from my family.
I totaled cars, blacked-out.
Had guns to my head.
Punched at while in my car by a ganger.
Gunned for money.

The eyes of God were still there.
Even though I was in sad shape.
God consoled me by working through my soul to create my music.
I wrote and sang songs of deliverance, just to give myself some hope.
To be encouraged for the Word and church again.
It finally started becoming closer to the Light.

I reread Romans 1:18–25, and some phrases stuck to my mind.
"Men are without excuse!" "All have sinned and fall short of the
     Glory of God" (Romans 3:23).
Romans 3:10, "There is no one righteous, no not one."
There is no one who understands and no one who seeks God.
God seeks you.

Left at this point, we would all be in a futile, hopeless position.
Something had to be done for us to have any chance of living in love,
     peace, and salvation!
Old Testament sacrifices were made for thousands of years.
In this imperfect world, payment is due for sins against society.

God made the ultimate sacrifice on the cross—Jesus, a gift to the
  world.
It is ours to accept humbly and with a penitent heart.
I am a testimony of His grace, love, and power.
"Trust in the Lord with all your heart and lean not unto thine own
  understanding.
In all ways acknowledge Him and He shall direct thy path" (Proverbs
  3:5).

Swansons

Grandpa Swanson was my favorite person to hang out with. He was a painter of houses and many Lake Vermilion cabins. He also was a strong, talented oil painter, and I have a few of them in our house. Our wall has a beautiful *Cutty Sark* ship and a cool cougar in the basement. Arthur Carl Gustaff Swanson had multiple blue ribbons with the state fair for art and won some money also!

He certainly loved his Blackie. Little did I know that he went through more than one Blackie in his life that I never figured out for many years. Dropping sugar cubes in his mouth was a regular for his coffee. Between some missing teeth, he let the sugar melt with the hot cup of coffee. Grandma Eva and Art would go to drop off eggs for milk at Cronholms and drop fresh eggs to others in town and the outer woods. When getting to the grocery store on a Saturday, Grandpa would always stop and talk with everyone, and Grandma just wanted to get the food and chicken feed and leave. She also would get a bit frustrated when Arthur would flirt with the women and keep them enjoying his sparkling eyes and sweet smile.

His favorite treats were black licorice, orange circus sponged nuts, and candy corn, thus, the missing teeth. The Cronholms were a nice old couple who had a milking cow herd but had one pretty old son who had some kind of mental disorder but was always at church with the family, and we could talk a little bit with him. But some people said to keep him away from girls or at least keep an eye on him.

Going fishing was my best time with Grandpa. We would take his old Ford truck over the gravel road to Vermilion until we came to a very steep hill. Parking at the top of the hill would show his dark

11

green-painted wooden boat near the shore. He hid the boat there to have a quick way to fish. We always caught fish. In the 1960s, it was much more subtle and quiet, and a lack of flying boats all over the lake. Very few fancy houses at that time. It was strictly for fishing! We'd come home and clean/fillet our fish, and Grandma would fry a delicious amount of catch for supper.

Horseshoes were an old Swedish game that I was taught at a young age. Grandpa was very good, and I got to be pretty good myself. He also taught me to play chess, and he would *not* let me win! Eventually, after a few years, I was able to win...I think. Again, his blue sparkling eyes and smiley face gave me some doubt and some hope.

He also taught me to drive a stick old truck out in the hayfields. I even drove on the country roads. Chopping wood for the house burner and an old stove that was garbage and woodburning made me some money. He would pay twenty-five cents for a cord after chopping and stacking the wood in the large garage. When I was in my teens, I looked around in the garage and found some holes, and in those holes were empty Skoal cans...chewing tobacco. Grandma surely knew he chewed but never near the house. She was a hard-core Christian.

I loved playing horseshoes and played with Blackie and would go fishing on Saturdays or sometimes on a weekday evening. I also would take a walk down to a spring where the water was always cold and delicious. Watching trees and looking in the air for eagles was always a way to walk and look around and smell the pine air with deep breaths. The spring waters were all over Cook and Vermilion, and the brown color was full of iron, and other springs were sweet clear water.

Barry, David, and I took a long walk to Great Uncle Milfred and Viola's stugatz (a small Swedish red cottage) one summer. It was probably about three to four miles in the woods. After going on the gravel roads about halfway, we had to make a sudden stop. There in the middle of the road was a giant bull moose. He didn't move, and they were willing to attack! So we waited awhile until the big dude slowly walked into the forest. We kept going to Carlson's stugatz in the middle of nowhere. It was a Swedish red house with a few rooms and a couple of bedrooms. It was also in bear territory. This was a period where there were not the amount of people on the lake or lodges. It was wild nature, peaceful, and beautiful that attracted me.

I also remember watching/babysitting Troy and Scott when they were like seven and four years old. Uncle Allen and Yvonne went out to Virginia, Minnesota, and the little house had a tiny kitchen, small, small living room, and one and one-half bedrooms. A block down in the little Cook City was a gas station that kept a black bear in a decently large cage. As other people would do, I would buy a bottle of pop for the bear, and he would down a bottle in less than twenty seconds. A funny memory with Troy was getting Penney's catalog and looking at the section that had women in their underwear and bras. Don't ever tell him I said this. Actually, go ahead and remind him!

When we went up north, it was in various ways. Barry and David were once already there when baby Lori, Mom, and I flew up to Duluth in a small two-engine plane. A storm built up quickly in the evening, and in the darkness, lightning caused most people to be fearful. The wind made it even worse and were rocking and shaking our plane around. Eventually, we made it, of course, and were picked up by Grandpa. Everyone was so happy that we were okay. I was excited to tell my brothers what an exciting trip we went through. They all smiled along with Grandpa but not Grandma as she had been in prayer after hearing about the storm. Similar to what my wife's mom Angie would have done.

Another way of going north was riding with Rube and Doris Stohlhammer from Chicago to bring us up. It was David who went up often, and I went a few times also. We would stop overnight in Ogema, Wisconsin, at Mabel's cow farm. She was Ingie's closest friend and a Stohlhammer. They had many kids like seven, and there were a few close to my age. It was fun to watch them milk the cows and spray some at each other for fun. The milk would be poured into a big container every early morning and evening. It was old ways in the early 1960s. I remember drinking totally unique but good fresh milk, and a quick mouse was no surprise, but I did jump. As I said,

Mabel was Ingie's best friend from Chicago days until she passed away in her upper 80s. They had been Maid of Honor when each of them married. They always kept in touch.

We first drove up in our small brown Oldsmobile, and I remember the three of us boys grabbing a pillow and blanket and crowding to our *beds*. I, being the youngest, would lay up behind the back window while Barry had the seats, and David put blankets on the floor. No seat belts at that time. In our second drive, we had a wood-sided Mercury wagon and had plenty of room. I think we stopped in the Dells overnight, which was rare. We also would go to Saint Paul and visit Milfred and Viola and John Carlson with Milfred being Grandma Eva's younger brother. Viola had a twin sister, Alberta, and both teachers were kindergarten teachers, and they both talked a lot. Milfred was an organist, a very good and well-known musician and music teacher at Bethel College.

I rode on a Greyhound bus for the first time by myself when I was eleven years old. I was driven by Dad to Chicago, and he set me off. The bus ride to Duluth took the whole night as the bus dropped off packages over and over with some people dropping off also as the ride was *boring*. We even stopped for snacks when the bus gassed up. I praised God when Allen picked me up and brought me to the Swanson castle outside of the city of Cook, Minnesota. Whew! I took another bus ride at fifteen years old and rode alone from Joliet all the way to Cook. This was kind of long, but I had books to read that helped.

Actually, I rode *again* mainly because I was given a painting job by King Arthur. There was a large area of boats that would be under rippled tin roofs and buildings usually for winter. The main building had sporting goods for fishing, boat preparation, and hunting materials. I primed and painted the main building, and I primed all eight to ten buildings for cold-weather protection.

My grandpa gave me lessons on things like where to start from top to bottom, fixing the paint, taking care of cleaning paint cans and safety on the ladders and scaffolding, and working on a hot roof, especially the main store. Oh, and I wore one of his used suspender painting clothes. I worked for about two weeks on the project. I started on the main store on the roof with sun-colored paint and usually hot days. By the end of my day, my eyes were dried out and sore from the brightness being reflected.

Grandma always prepared a delicious lunch with her handmade Swedish rye bread and salami or ham or fresh chicken, and I always had a full coffee in my thermos. I'd get down from the roof or ladder and walk down a block just off the main highway where there was a picnic table to relax and eat (and sneak a smoke because I was *cool*.) It took a good week to paint the main structure. Grandpa dropped me off and picked me up at the same time every day, and we'd talk going home, clean our brushes, burn out a couple of buckets, and clean ourselves before Grandma would have a fantastic supper.

I figured out that coming home from work, he had not only a paint smell but a Skoal chew smell also, and he hid the cans from Eva in holes in the garage. I am sure Grandma knew and didn't like it, but she seemed to avoid it in front of any of us kids. She was a super-dedicated Christian who was in Scripture and prayer daily. I and my family were very appreciative of her faith and action. Teaching Sunday school, preparing for presentations of Christ, and working in every aspect of the church and with an indigenous tribe nearby in Togo every summer. She is also the one who took care of three large veggie gardens and multiple flower gardens all around the house.

Add that she was the one who took care of the chickens and ducks and stayed close to the baby chicks in an incubator in the upper garage every spring/early summer. I loved watching and helping them grow as they were so sweet, cute, and needy. Add that she canned everything she grew for the many months after summer. Green beans, peas, beets, lettuce, cabbage (potatoes were for Grandpa), blueberries, and strawberries (as long as I wasn't picking), and I loved when she used the rhubarb and added custard to eat that when it was still hot. So delicious! My favorite pie ever! One year, the sweet lady sent me a large couple of cinnamon biscuits with a birthday card. The biscuits had gotten large marshmallows in the middle before baking, and inside the hollow middle when I was eating it, there was a five-dollar bill for me. It meant a lot.

Grandpa had no problem eating chicken from the best fresh food possible, but he didn't like chopping off their heads and watching the headless bodies wander around with blood dripping. Eva was the one who did most of the chopping heads, plucking feathers, cleaning the body, and cooking the meat. I was given the morning job of feeding leftover veggies and chicken pellets for food over the coop ground and water in the tin water feeders. They loved me for that. There were usually a few mallard females that laid some big brown eggs, which I liked even better than the chicken eggs. The roosters, who liked to chase young strangers as I, forced me to turn around and chase them away. I won some and lost some.

Now collecting the chicken eggs from their nest was not the easiest for me to do. Some left their small square bin, and it was great. However, many wanted to sit on their nest and didn't want to be messed with. I was pecked many times until I started to use a stick to flip them out of their nest. They all would be very loud and disgusted by balking with some smoke coming from their heads. I also ended up busting a few eggs every once and a while.

I was able to work for a well-known Hall of Fame cowboy who retired to a farm of wild horses. The Benns lived in a modest cabin mostly surrounded by cold delicious spring creeks, and they had many wild horses in the field. Sidney Benn and his wife were good friends of my grandparents, which was why I learned about wild horses and got to work with a wild young one who would try to step on my foot if I didn't keep track of the cutie. Sidney started helping me to carefully work with the wild blonde girl and learning to lead and rope her and carefully lead her. I would not close an eye, and I only helped there for two weeks, so I didn't get a chance to ride her but did get closer especially when I fed her sugar cubes and/or apple pieces.

I had to be paying attention to her very carefully as she liked to stomp on my foot if my eyes looked away. We got to know each other pretty well though my two weeks weren't enough to ride her. When I treated her to some sugar cubes or an apple when she was a good girl, I could almost see the blond smile at me.

Driving a tractor that had a bad seat, make that no seat at all, just a steel piece that used to hold a seat! Bumping along, I made it be that I did *not* fall back on the steel piece. I would drag logs of pinewood and birch branches in different areas and keep fires and smoke going so some of the wild horses could come close to chill out and away from the nasty *horse* flies, pun intended.

Back to the Swanson's one hundred acres of wild woods, I usually slept in one of the upstairs bedrooms, and one time I shared the small bed with my dad when all of us were there. Three bedrooms with Grandma and Grandpa in a room with a big bed, a long closet for clothes to hang, and a small area looking out the window across a field that deer always came through after supper. I also would sneak into the small area and play with Grandpa's guitar.

There was a small room downstairs with a large window right next to the front porch. There were many Swedish things like the orange-painted horses with delicate careful colors of paint stripes. These were, of course, by the painter/artist Arthur. He also carved some strange-looking characters that were a little scary when I was really young but very cool when I was a little older. Not sure how we could fit five or six of us in the last couple of beds.

Early on, when the only kids were the three boys coming up with the parents, the only usable toilet was a small red biffy between the garage and the chicken coop. The need to go out at night was a bit scary to go out by the chicken coop. We could put on bright lights on the way to the pooper, but the sound of coyotes or wolves or a screaming bobcat kind of scared me a lot anyway. Also, you would always be aware of a bear coming through or other animals looking for food.

So at that time, to protect our safety, we boys were all given a Folgers Coffee can for us to pee into and dump them out in the sewage field the next morning. It created a great smell! There was a toilet in the basement, but for quite a while, they had to be careful to flush very often so the sewage wouldn't overflow on the way to the field. Eventually, around 1965 maybe, Arthur built a new room for a new toilet and connected it to the water well and septic connection. Even then when we took a weekly bath, we could only have the hot water up to ten to twelve inches.

Back to the downstairs bedroom that I slept in by myself. It would be a very chilling place initially, especially in an area that would be pitch-black outside. Then again there would be open skies that shined an unbelievable amount of stars and moon. Inside the backdoor of the house was like a modest-sized porch with screen windows in the summer. Inside was an old-fashioned wringer, which was operated by a hand-turned crank for pressing the water out of the washed clothes. Long ropes out front would have the clothes dried out in the sweet pine air and surrounded by multiple flower beds.

On the back door porch is where I would keep stocked chopped wood and bags of dog biscuits for Blackie. Wisely, I had to try one out, and it really wasn't bad...if you were really hungry. The garage was filled with cords of the chopped wood that was mostly done by me. On the outer back door was a large sliced-up scratch of a bear trying to get inside the back door. That was a thought I had every night because I was next to the windows, which would be easy for a bear to come from the wide opened forest across the street and up the porch steps and break into me and put me away, but I am still here. The mind can really mess with not only kids but adults also.

Another weird happening for the young boy that I was came from an old man named Johnny who lived about a mile away in a tiny probably one-room house and a little kitchen and fireplace. How he survived, I will never know, but Johnny would often be wobbling down the road with a sweeper to clean the road and hold himself up. He was a longtime serious alcoholic. I would see him while being outside sometimes, and he would say hello and wave, and I would do the same back to him. I felt really sad about the guy and so was Grandpa. Grandpa Art would stop when seeing him going eight to ten miles toward the town for more alcohol but picked him up and sat the poor guy in the back of the truck. In town, we would wait for him when he was coming back to make sure he was okay and would get back to his small cabin. Even though I had short talks with Johnny, Grandma told me to stay away from him, so I avoided him, but I was not afraid of the man. It was just my grandma being like a hen taking care of her chick.

Another weird thing was my great-uncle Einar who was married to my great-aunt Naomi, who was a bit weird and my grandma's sister. Einar was a round-bellied Swede who could play the guitar well along with Grandpa, and some adults thought he was funny, but I thought he was a little strange around the many, many kids who would be around Cook, Minnesota, in the summers. When families would gather at the Swanson's mansion, he would make weird sounds just to scare kids. I remember one time in the evening and with multiple cousins, most of us were in the front yards playing catch, tag, or just goofing around or talking.

Suddenly, across the road, there was heard a loud bear coming through the woods. Then we started to hear mean growling, and many kids started screaming and telling adults what was happening. When the growling got even louder, all of us were scared. Then running out of the woods was Einar coming after us all while many parents were just laughing, and a few were not. Grandma was not; she didn't like it.

Naomi was a bit strange and was Grandma Eva's sister. She looked a little like a famous painting with the farmer and rarely smiled in pictures. Stoned faced. She rarely smiled at all, and her husband was just the opposite. It surprised me when Naomi came to stay with us as Mom was in the hospital with Lori. Her hair went down past her rear after she washed it, but then she just kept it tied around her head. She was a bit scary for me as a young kid. She helped with all the meals and always had them ready for Barry, David, and me. What was freaky was she would just stare with her chin on her hand, mainly at David while eating breakfast. It was uncomfortable for poor David. She mainly just stared for the whole time without talking. Maybe that is why I, as a little boy, carried with me to hate when our dogs or cat Romeo would stare at me while eating.

Back to Minnesota

Some last experiences happened when I walked down a half mile from Grandpa Arthur's house and turned into a dirt road toward the woods just to see what was in there. I found lots of blueberries and ate a bunch as well as a paper bag full of the sweet fruit. I found a spring of water on the side of a road and stunned a doe as we stared at each other for a while before she said goodbye and slowly walked away. There was a small beat-up wooden house a little farther down the road that wasn't worth going into because it looked like it would fall apart at any moment.

I turned to walk back when I stopped to get some more blueberries. As fast as a snap, I stepped through rusty car parts, and all of a sudden, many amounts of bees came flying out, and they were not happy! After the first sting, I took off running as fast as I could. I still got stung a few times before I was away from soldier bees. Since I wanted to get back home, I decided to cut through the big field that goes to the house.

As I got close to halfway, I started getting wet and kept going as I didn't think it would last. As I went forward, I started smelling like *fweet* (a Swedish word) in the air. When I finally got back, Grandma was out in one of the gardens. When she saw me coming, she started to smile.

Eva asked, "What happened to you?"

I said, "I was just checking things out in the woods and was stung by bees and cut through the field, and now I stink!" She told me to put my clothes aside and hopped me into a large water barrel that collected the rain to wash the poop/pee crap from me as well as my damaged clothes. After getting that done, Grandma told me about baby kitties that Buster had a week ago outside. She said they had to drown them in the same barrel I *cleaned* myself in!

When I was an eighth grader, I asked Mom, and Mom asked Grandma if I could bring a good friend, John B., to come up with me. Even though Grandma said when someone else brought up a friend before, it didn't work very well, it is okay. So we took the bus, of course, and when we got there, we were doing all right. We played an old football game that was Uncle Allen's game. We were able to get into Virginia when we both stole a small knife and had lunch. We got to fish one day with Grandpa, but on the fourth day, it was getting boring, and we got in a fight, and Johnny wanted to leave.

It was so bad for him that he took his suitcase and started walking down the road. So Grandpa picked him up, and they said John should call home and let his parents know he would be coming home early. So we set things up for him to take the Greyhound. We were still friends but kind of went our own ways in different high schools. I still text every once in a while on Facebook. He ended up being a sports reporter on the radio.

When I was in the army, Illinois National Guard, I did a lot of walking to get ready for a two-week gruesome long workout physically and would play war out in the woods doing army field training exercises. I had my back pack and filled it with stones and walked three to four miles before I turned around to go back home. On the way back, I would stop by a small set up that had running spring water that was super cold and delicious. After the hot day and extra weight and sweating, that water was precious, and I was ready to go!

Anderson Grandparents

I must admit I had super grandparents on each side. Total Swedish background for as many generations that I know. Grandpa Sam and Ella Anderson lived just about eight blocks from my house. They were close to Saint Dennis, super teacher Charlotte Walker, and the old high school where Ella went to high school.

Sam fought in WWI in France with the army infantry. I remember when he took me up to the attic to look through some of his memorabilia and old newspapers, Nazi officer clothes, diaries, and some German weapons. I think the vast majority of family photos and things from the attic went to the Richters. They were the only other family connection. It also could have been stolen with some of the big stuff.

One thing that caught my eye was a Victrola record player. Asking him to explain what in the world it was put a soft smile on his face and made him giggle as he brought out some, no many, 78rpm records from the WWI time of music. He was always a strong Christian, from a teenager to his death, and always helped people in need, but the old music was a surprise. I begged him to start playing some music from the late 1910s to '20s.

He revved it up and let me choose a couple of records, and the first piece to come out was "Over There" by George Cohen. I got up, and in a second, I was marching on the old wooden floor, keeping the beat like a little soldier. Another record was "K-K-K-Katy" which stimulated Grandpa to get up and start to march and sing along with the song. The Victrola had to be started by hand (if I think of it correctly). It had a black color and was shaped like an orange cone on a highway. It also had the symbol of a terrier mix dog named Nipper with black ears and the rest white. "Sneaky Pete" was a jazz record I heard as well as Bessie Smith singing "Baby Won't You Please Come Home." The scratchy sound reminded me of my own portable little GE player that always bugged my mom at night.

Later, he told me that he kept a diary he began in his teens before the big war. He pointed out stacks of "Daily Aide for the Secretary." I was able to collect a vast majority of his books from 1919 to the 1980s when he passed away. I was deeply frustrated when he died while I was with the National Guard at Fort Campbell and didn't hear the information until after the funeral as they wouldn't let me go anyway. I was frustrated, angry, and sad.

He was someone I was able to see most all of my days until he went to heaven. Ella married Sam before he crossed the Atlantic, and he had his sweetheart in his diary for sure, waiting in prayer to get back home. Grandma Ella was a very sweet, small lover of Jesus, dedicated to the church and totally providing for her family.

Great-grandma Wenberg had a room downstairs that was connected to Sam and Ella's room by a long hall that was used for all their hanging clothes. The whole house was filled with dark Ebony wood that was solid and stayed solid and perfect from 1898 to today, February 13, 2023. Great-granny was able to walk in and out of her bedroom but liked to sneak up to the attic.

Grandpa said, "Let me know if she is starting to go upstairs. It's way too dangerous for her to walk up the steep steps."

There were many antique objects and things that were hers that she wanted to take care of and remember. Actually, I still have the trunk she came over from Sweden with, and she was never to see some family members again except via letters. All my ancestors on both sides of my branch of the family were from Sweden. I'd like to go back four to six generations in our family and dig into what they were about. I know at least three to four generations were filled with Christianity.

There was an old radio about five feet high with the sound coming from the bottom half. The dial was usually on CBS, WGN, or Moody Bible for the main stations. Actually, when I was about six years old this radio with multiple bulbs in the back didn't work at all. So I started to look at the back bulbs and messed with them, trying to tighten loose ones and unscrew tight ones and then tighten them again in their sockets. Rocking the radio back and forth a couple of times, I tried to see if it would work. *It did!* A miracle? Lucky move?

I remember when I was about eight years old listening to a boxing match with Sonny Listen and a young Cassius Clay. Young Clay won the fight.

Great-granny Wenberg had a rocking chair in front of the radio where she would listen to old music, old church songs, and the news. One day I came over to her and saw her colored veins in her hands and arms, and she was rocking away. I slowly, carefully walked up to her and put my hand softly on hers just to say hello. There was a smile on her face. Then very quickly she slapped her hand on mine! It scared me at first and made me jump a little, but her smile settled me down. Others just laughed, and I smiled. Later, when she passed away, she was said to have raised her arm and pointed to the sky, letting people know she was with Jesus. I was not allowed to go to her funeral. I was thought to be too young to come and see the dead old one lying in a casket and people crying.

One thing that happened after she passed away and after her funeral was a nightmare to me. A few days later, Sam and Ella asked me to come to their house for the night and watch the Cubs game against San Francisco. Happily, I accepted the invitation, and when I was brought over and walked into the house, we turned on the game.

After some treats and playing a couple of games like Candy Land, I asked Grandpa, "Where will I sleep?"

He brought me into the bedroom of Great-grandma. It gave me terrible thoughts.

He pulled up the blankets for me, and Grandma gave me a kiss. I had a hard time falling asleep in *her* bed. I was afraid she might be coming down those steep steps of the attic. After I fell asleep, I heard steps just outside the bedroom, slowly and softly walking down the steps. I tiptoed to the squeaky door and opened it carefully. There she was at the *top* of the steps staring at me. She looked spooky! I tried to scream, but nothing came out, so I ran through the clothes closet to Sam and Ella's bedroom, and they were both gone! I ran out where the TV was on but without sound, and I saw Sam sitting on the sofa.

I asked, "Grandpa, did you hear who was making the noise?"

He didn't answer me, but instead walked to the kitchen and turned the light on. That is when I looked toward the kitchen, and what did I see? The other side of the sofa was taken by the *head* of Great-grandma with her white hair sticking out all over! I started crying and pulled the blanket over *my* head and tightened the rest of the covers to keep me safe the rest of the night.

Back to reality, Grandpa Sam worked for Gerlach-Barlow Works creating different kinds of cards. It was the largest of its kind and was built in 1908. I am not sure when Grandpa started working there, but it was since I was born for sure. When I was about five and up, he would bring cards home and use them to write letters to give a spirit of hope to soldiers in WWII, the Korean War, Vietnam, and others. Building encouragement and blessings, he always lifted everyone's hope.

He was constantly involved with just about everything in the Swedish Baptist Church on Jackson Street, which was in a very multicultural area. There was a rockin' Black Baptist Church right around the corner too, with great singing going on there! Sam sang in the choirs, was a head deacon for many, many years, and helped anyone who came for support spiritually...anyone! He was the lead elder and would visit anyone in the hospital or senior living. Back then many of the old-timers were not treated very well in the senior homes, so visitors would be a blessing for them and the visitors. Mom worked in one of those homes after getting her nursing license in her late 40s before working at St. Joseph Hospital.

Sam would always walk into our house with a specific whistle, which was kind of like people today have a certain ringtone so you know who they are. Also, when Sam would smell something cooking, he'd say, "Ohhh, it stinks really good," and always, "Is anyone home?" He just liked to see how things were, give out any news he had, and drop off some things. Irritation is what Mom would think sometimes because he came often. He once took me to a Cubs game, which was the team he watched whenever he could. Even though I was and am a White Sox fan, I loved guys like Ernie Banks, who was one of the coolest and greatest hitters ever from Chicago.

He also gave me my first car which was a brown Oldsmobile, I think, and I drove it until it died. He gave me another car, his old Rambler, which actually ran pretty well. It had three shifts that were set on the right side of the steering wheel. I had never worked a shift car except for once with Grandpa Arthur's truck a couple of times. I had that car for a year before I hit a tree by Dellwood Park, and it was no longer worth fixing.

I was close enough to the apartment I shared with my dad to just walk home and let the city truck bring the car to the junkyard. In our apartment was a seven-foot sailfish, which my dad finally got after wanting it his whole life. We kept it in an open decorated box with Christmas lights during winter and even longer. Anyway, it was not long before I bought my red 1965 Mustang with the money I was given from Grandpa and Grandma Swanson after they went to Jesus. This car I loved and had it for a long time especially compared to the last cars I had.

During my middle school days, I came to see Grandma Ella and Sam quite often. Supper was often chicken with gravy, sometimes a type of beef or meatloaf, and Sunday might be a ham along with her creamed peas. Yum, my favorite. Ice cream would often be for dessert as Sam would bring up a pint of vanilla from Weber's Ice Cream which was only three blocks away. What Grandma would do was open the pint container's sides and slice the ice cream with a knife to create equally sized squares for everyone. You've never seen that before, I bet.

We would play checkers or a couple of different card games and something called "Buttons, Buttons?" We also would hear some Scripture and pray just before eating. I am sad that I haven't continued that tradition with my family. I was used to being alone for many years before getting married. Then my wife and children were almost always having sports practice or my wife was late from work or at Grandma Angie's (her mom) giving kids piano lessons.

While I was attending Kelvin Grove, I was doing things for Sam because Grandma was starting to get confused and needed help at times. I would cut the grass every weekend and collect the cut grass in a spot way back in the yard. I brought Grandma cookies that I baked occasionally until she was getting too bad to go to church, making little sense and having a blank look on her face. She was talking one day at the kitchen table about her motorcycle in the attic (there was never a motorcycle in the attic). Another day she was yelling at Sam about someone coming for supper and madly saying, "I don't want no ——r in my house!" When she was the *real* Ella, she was the sweetest person around. Her brain at this point was losing blood, and it totally took away who she really was. She could no longer be around anyone and be able to connect to them. Sam took care of her as much as he could because he was a totally loving, God-led person!

I remember coming over to Grandpa's to help clean up things in the house. Looking at Grandma's face and into her eyes, she looked like she was controlled by a demonic being. I think she was already dead and in heaven before the body was buried anyway. It must have been hard on Sam, but he was so strong. "I can do all things through Christ who strengthens me." His spiritual guidance all his life allowed him to continue walking with Jesus for the rest of his life.

Sam told me one day when we were talking about his three brothers who were all still alive. Uncle Bob was my favorite by far because he was the one I saw all the time. His son was Wendell Anderson who was a professor and missionary with his wife and family for years in the Philippines. He came back to the States and worked under Billy Graham in Minnesota.

When I was in fourth or fifth grade, I wanted to get a "Danny Boy" doll and become a ventriloquist! When Uncle Bob heard about it, he dug into his old stuff at his house and brought me a 6×6 booklet, which had all kinds of information as to how to be a ventriloquist. It was from the early 1900s, and I was excited. I worked with Danny often, when not doing sports, and started using the directions in the book. I ended up being pretty good to start with it.

One night after Sunday church, we came home and had grilled cheese with hot chocolate. While eating, we watched *Twilight Zone* on our black-and-white TV. The story was about a ventriloquist and his doll. In the beginning, he put on a good show with his *Danny*. However, as the story went on, Danny started taking over the man until Danny was totally in charge of being the ventriloquist himself, and the man became a worthless, stupid doll.

Well, I was not too crazy about my Danny Boy after that. Every time I looked at him, I thought about the *Twilight Zone* episode. I no longer kept him in my bedroom. It was hard for me to fall asleep with him there in my room. So what I did right away was find a spot at the top of our winding steps, *across* from the start of our hall, a somewhat triangular flat small place that Danny would fit on just perfectly. I figured he would not be able to get out unless he wanted to fall down the steps…and then I'd at least hear the crash. Anyway, I no longer was a ventriloquist, and now I'm not sure what ever happened to him. Maybe he did get up and left to go to someone else willing to work with him. I hope it all went well.

Another thing Sam told me about is where my dad was born. It was a house that was only about a block and a half from our house on Seventh Street! It was a small house just above a creek (the one we kids played in—it was a long, winding creek), and the house was next to Rex's Garage. Then Grandpa told about how Ella lost one of her babies around 1924. It wasn't uncommon to lose a baby back then. A black horse pulling a black buggy would come, and the baby was taken to a funeral home.

On the lighter side of things, when I was like six years old, Mom gave me money to get us both a peppermint ice cream sundae with hot fudge, whipped cream, and a cherry on top. *Yum!* I actually took a stack of Sam's many diaries after he passed away. I found a page in a diary where he had written my Weber's Ice Cream story! So when little me walked seven blocks excited for the tasty, upcoming dream, I walked into Weber's and walked right up to the high counter. I waited and waited and spoke a couple of times, but I guess as short as I was they couldn't see me. Sad and a bit mad, I walked out and down the two to three blocks to get Grandpa to help me. "Well, of course, I'll help you, Dougie!" He drove us down in the Rambler, which he would give me many years later, and explained to the lady behind the counter who was making the sundaes. The lady felt sad about the cute little me, and I only had to pay for one sundae…mine was free! Grandpa drove me home (oh, that is why he drove his car), and Mom and I slowly enjoyed the delicious taste of a prize.

Elementary School

Oh, I remember so well what my long-lived house was like when I grew up. It was at least an eighty-year-old house when I was only five years old. Our garage, which was a block behind the house, was tilted a bit and didn't have an entry door at all. It is a place where I—with my best friend, who was also five years old—made a plan to go and examine what was happening there next store where Gene lived.

We saw that Gene, the mom, and his two sisters had gone right before we approached the house. Since we had such brilliant brains, we decided to walk to the back door and knock a few times, and we found the house was empty. So we slowly opened the door and peeked around both sides before entering. How smart we were, eh? Toy trucks and cars were around the kitchen floor, and we messed with them for a short time. Then with some fruit on the table for something to eat! The grapes looked delicious and tasted even better. A banana was not bad either.

After that, the eyes of JM fell upon a large jar of beautiful, tempting, delicious peanut butter! As he opened the jar, there was a strange sound in the house. We were scared. Stopping in silence, we heard a very weird sound again. They didn't have a dog. What could it be? So we slowly tiptoed into the family room and saw or heard nothing, but then the sound was even louder. Was it an outdoor animal, some kind of monster, or a ghost?

So we went to the next small room door that barely opened and peeked inside. There, snoring on a small bed was Mr. Bonrough. Well, what do you think? We both quickly ran back through the kitchen but took the jar of peanut butter, ran from the left open door, and shot over the ground to my land. We ended up in the garage with our breathing going almost as fast as our hearts.

Eating the peanut butter and wondering how much trouble we would get into, JM scooted on a cross beam up high in the garage and held the jar while sitting and swinging his leg as his face was creamed with the *food*. He was daring me to cross over with him, but I left that for the baby raccoons I have. While we were singing some dumb song, there was a big amount of glass hitting the cement hard floor. JM was crying and yelling for help. He was bleeding from his head, and I ran to our house and told Mom what happened. Ingie called over to Mrs. Major who was totally freaked out. JM was taken to the Lockport Clinic where my aunt Alberta worked on stitches for his head. Needless to say, it was a long while before my friend and I could get together again.

We had a very large yard in our backyard, and there were many fruit trees. A peach tree was just outside the back tiny kitchen door. We had four large apple trees, and they were all different types. One was for nothing but baking yummy pies while the others were sweet to eat, but cleaning up the rotten apples was a pain in the butt.

The inside of our old house was okay. We had a dining room for the seven of our family eventually and was a good place for kids to play and adults to play Rook. Our dining room table was where I stole a dollar bill as a six-year-old. Money was needed for food, and we used it week by week. I did ask my mom if I could have some pennies to get some candy when one could get two pieces of candy for a penny! But Mom said no. (I didn't know the dollar was for our milk.) However, when no one was around, I crawled to the table and just put my arm up but couldn't reach it. I didn't want Mom to see me and kept trying to grab it without looking over the table! Finally, I gave that up, stood up with my eye on the dollar, grabbed it, and ran across the street to the dairy store.

Thinking all was well, I skipped into the dairy to the ice cream/candy store where the big lady was there to take my wishes. She was a very nice lady and gave me a root beer float for my birthday a week ago. I asked for a float again for my *birthday*. She gave me a big smile and said, "Dougie, you had a birthday last week!" Oh well, when

I put down the dollar and started pointing out all the candies and came away with two hundred candies, I was in pleasure eating two pieces until I got to the front door.

Mom was standing at the front door waiting. Oh, Mom knew the nice lady, of course, and must have talked with her about the situation. Up the winding stairs we go, and Mom spanked me with her wide red belt. (I never forgot it.) She explained why she spanked me, and it really wasn't hard slaps. I know that she didn't like it, and I think it hurt her more than me. The worst part of the deal is my brothers got to eat the candy, and we didn't have any milk for the week! Shame on me.

Across Seventh Street, there was a large amount of trees and fields and a winding creek that was multiple miles long. Tracking through the water in the summer was a fun time to set traps for minnows as well as crayfish. Using coffee cans and catching by hand or a tight net was fun. I often would bring them home and a couple of times or more, I put them in the bathtub. For some reason, no one else was crazy about it. They just thought I was crazy. It was something to play with in the tub, no? Well, I did smell quite fishy when I got out of the tub and the towel stunk too. Sorry, Mom!

We would go from a small island, across Madison Street and across the weed-filled field. Often we would stop to cool our feet and splash in the creek on the way to the tunnel. It was about six to eight feet high and water ran to a large concreted collection of water. Storms of rain would make the creek run much more strongly and could be very dangerous at times. The tunnel was also an easy way to get minnows but not during storms. Fishing in the concrete area was a good way to catch small fish.

Swimming was also done by area kids. Not a bright idea though. There was even a strange, older kid named Malcolm who would even jump in during the cold when there were big chunks of ice and he was always smoking. This is the same guy who was a couple of years older than my brother Dave who came into our yard, and my brother David got in a fight with him and sent him away.

There was a small island going across the street and walking through the weeds. I would go there after getting my first BB rifle and shot at cans and probably bottles. On a shiny, soft windy day, listening to the birds, I saw a girl who was walking across a long way on the field from me. She looked tiny being far away, but I did recognize her from fourth grade, and I was a fifth grader. Without thinking, I couldn't do any harm if I aimed my rifle up in the air and pulled the trigger. Could I? This had to be at least seventy-five yards away, *but yes!* It hit her! She looked around and saw who I was and I saw how she was crying and felt terrible.

The next day was a Saturday, and my papa was home. Playing in my bedroom with a small ball and self-built rim, I heard my dad talking to someone outside. Looking out a window from upstairs, I saw it was a cop! Being called to be outside, I was ready to poop in my pants. The girl's dad was the policeman (which I didn't know), and we had a talk about the danger of doing such a thing. The cop had to take my rifle, and I would have to go down to the station with Dad the next day. Going downtown, I was asked to apologize and agree to never do anything like this again. I agreed I would never fire at anyone. My rifle had a tag on it by the way like it was about a real crime person, and I took the weapon back home with my head down, and my dad just put his arm around me...

Off from the dining room was a large outside screen around the whole porch. My dad eventually had a single bed there. When I was about ten, I had a baseball dartboard with parts showing single through a home run, strike out and walks, fly outs, and ground outs. I would get my baseball cards out and put them in batting order and write down each batter for each team. I loved it! One day Lori came on the porch and was a six-year-old and liked to follow me around. She always wanted what I wanted, but she was a good kid and grew up as a great one. But when she irritated me while playing, I asked her to hold out her arm in front of the dartboard to see how close I could get. I really don't remember, but I don't think I meant to hit her arm with the sharp dart. Yes, it hurt, and she ran out crying to Mom, who comforted Lori with a scowling face toward me.

Off of the porch, there was a big door leading down limestone steps to the basement. It was dark with little light and plenty spooky at times. For quite a long time, we had coal dumped into a section of the basement and was kind of fun to watch. There was a small pantry with all limestone and one dull light bulb. Canned tomatoes and fruit were in there. Just before going in, there was a crawl opening under the house, and I would have nothing to do with that. When we got back from church in the evening, we would watch Alfred Hitchcock and/or *Twilight Zone*. Barry, David, and I took turns putting coal in the furnace. Of course, I was the one to go down during *Twilight Zone*, and in the darkness, I got out of there as fast as I could. When I was a little older, I remember being called to put a new fuse in the fuse box, and I often got shocked.

In our living room, we had an old blue sofa, a table Dave made in high school, and I think one chair. On cold days, we would all like to lay on the floor with our feet lying on the heat vent and watching TV. We had three large windows angled behind our black-and-white TV and got a color eventually. Those windows remind me of a nasty tornado in Lockport.

Ingie was in the hospital, and I don't remember why the rest of us were at home. There was a warning, and the tornado hit fast! Barry and David were the first down the basement, and Howie carried Lori because she was just a baby. After Dad pushed me to go ahead, we made it just in time as all three windows came blasting and smashed against the far wall, saving us from serious damage.

After spending time in the very dark basement, the storm went through, and we had no electricity for two weeks. Our roof needed replacement, and we lost multiple trees with a large pear tree that was taken out of the ground and stuck upside down about thirty yards past the garage. Most of our backyard was a jungle of branches and trees that took two weeks to clean up. Many houses were destroyed, and St. Dennis Church was messed up and needed to be fixed. The tornado was around 110 mph and in a funnel shape.

My castle school was only three and a half blocks from home. In good weather, I often walked upon the rocks in the creek. In the end, it was a very steep hill to walk up and get ready for school. I remember my first-grade teacher because she liked me and was very pretty. We had a twist dance contest, and I was the best. Sadly she got married at the end of the year and didn't return. That was okay because I was always a short one with the pictures and had pretty girls close to me.

Throwing kisses at girls and from others was fun in class. Vicki B. and Karen S. were the ones who went back and forth with the blowing kisses. Going home one day, my mom was taking care of baby Lori, and she still had the weight on her, and her wedding ring wouldn't fit. Because of that, I started to look in her dresser where she hid a candy bar or two and found a ring on her dresser. Well, she couldn't wear it, so I picked it up and brought it to school.

The next day, I had a special offer to give Karen S. a ring to be my wife! She took the ring, put it on, and was delighted. Later that day after school, Mom got a phone call from Mrs. S. She was supposedly having a very cute and sweet speech about the situation. I think Ingie got a kick out of it too and got the ring back the next morning. It is hard to look back and see how goofy I was back in the day and probably not much different today.

Going home from school one day, I had an idea (scary). I planned on going off the street along the creek to the big curve and staying there lying down on the gravel. I wanted to freak someone out. One car beeped. Another person yelled at me to get out of the way, but the third car stopped, and an old lady came kind of running to see if I was okay. I jumped up and told her I just fell asleep after a long time at school and ran all the way home. A real bright child I was, eh?

I actually played the cornet in fourth to seventh grade. It was my brother Barry's instrument originally. The band would meet in the basement next to the boiler. Not the best place to play but there was no other choice. We had a great teacher who did a lot for Central and Kelvin Grove, and he built state-winning, excellent music. I was taking weekly lessons from a cool guy and got pretty good. Going to the county and state I was doing solo and worked with a partner. The ribbons and medals I earned went from third place to first place solo.

In seventh grade, during Veterans Day, I made a mistake however. Karen S. was at one side of the stage to play the first part, and I was giving the echo, but I was in a different key and had to go through the whole thing like that. I was embarrassed, and I didn't play after seventh grade. It was more because of flag football, basketball, and baseball really though.

I remember being challenged by a couple of different boys in the fourth to fifth area. I am not sure where it came from, but Mark P. jumped at me from behind and knocked me down. Never heard why it was done, but he was always a cool friend for the rest of my years. Also, a new student came to Central, and I challenged Phil to a fight at the top of the steep hill after school. I had a chain that I was swinging to hit him with, and we ended up talking together and were friends for the rest of our childhood. We did kind of like each other's girlfriends though.

Back in early grades, there were kids all over the place. Every block of every section of Lockport was loaded with kids. Within two blocks, there were the Krumlinde's four kids, Bodorf's three kids, one older Fowler girl, a couple of Reardons, scary older Malcolm, and the Rheinholz Gronholz and his weird sister, Ingrid. Ages went from five to seventeen, and we boys were totally outnumbered.

Steal the bacon was my favorite as we had a two-foot cement/stone wall on each side of the street and above the large tunnel. Whatever we used as the bacon would be placed in the middle of the street. One person would number each kid and call out a number loudly. So number 2s would come out and try to get the bacon without being touched. I kicked butt with my speed! We would play hide-and-seek on one side of the street. Of course, we would play tag and kick the bucket. Another favorite of mine was playing red light/green light. Again, I was good at it because I could get farther on the green light without being caught.

As Jeff M. and I grew out of the old games, Mr. Irish Gerrity taught fourth and fifth grade, and we always got to go out on the large stones gravel for an infield and play kickball. In the summer, we would get multiple guys together and start playing baseball. This infield is where I learned to be a super defensive player because you never know how the hit ball would bounce. Home runs would be hitting one on the road, but if you were fast, you could try to go as far as you could. If you broke a window, we all would go home quickly.

The guys I remember the most were Jeff M., of course, the McCarthy brothers, Tim B., Larry B., Dana, Odle brothers, Pez bros, B. Bazoo and J. Bowers. We would be out early morning, get a quick lunch, or go to the nearby Gable's bar to get some candy, baseball cards, chips, and a pop if we had money. If we went home for lunch, we would be back again until we *had* to come home. These were the days when a town with kids all over would set everything up for teams. There was no adult bossing around, and we took care of any fights ourselves.

As a fifth-grade basketball player attending Kelvin Grove Middle School, I would be going in with the big kids. As a player, I was like a mosquito at night as I was little, quick, hard to get, and irritating to an opposing team because I could dribble well and steal the ball often and score! It was these skills I looked forward to showing off in the big fifth graders against the sixth graders game in front of a gym full of people and the coaches would be watching.

Fear can be like a dirty cancer as it will grow and grow until it consumes you if nothing is done about it. Anger and frustration can also do this as well. Confidence and practice should have been for me. Sometimes for young kids as well as adults it is difficult to choose what to do. That very day I chose to be afraid and struggled with even playing. I lied when I told our team I would play. I told no one of my fear. Even the day we would play I told Mr. Gerrity I would be there as they counted on me for playing point guard. I didn't go. I felt ashamed. I was hiding in the garage and actually felt sick. My stomach was jumping around choosing not to go. It hurt for the whole weekend. However, no one said anything but that they missed having me there and that we were clobbered.

When I went to sixth grade basketball, I was having a blast against many different teams and had a very cool coach. His name was Roger Gifford and was a senior at Lewis College but a little older than most and married. A good guy when he left we would still go over to his house and talk or…watch a basketball game.

Back to school, I was part of a *friend* to light papers on fire in the garbage can that was in the lower level boy's bathroom. After smoke was seeping up the stairs, we were brought to the principal, and I was the first one smacked in the butt with a firm wooden paddle. It was allowed in those days. I didn't cry, but it was the last time I got into any trouble. Kind of. On a good *side* was Christmas time, and all students from first grade to fifth grade would gather in the wide open area on the main floor, singing Christian Christmas songs as well as Santa/Rudolph songs. We would go to our classroom and pass around candy canes and chocolates to each kid and do some handmade project to bring home. Singing Christian songs today are against the public school law, and our country has been in a wrong direction, and most of the world is in the same way.

I had a teacher named Mrs. Mehnken who taught second- and third-grade math. Every time she walked into the room, we all had to have our hands folded on the middle of our old, *old*, wooden desks and say sweetly to her, "Good morning, Mrs. Mehnken." Many times I would say instead, "Good morning, Mrs. Monkey," and everyone would blast out laughing, except Mrs. Mehnken. She would keep me after school every time I said that *phrase*. Multiple math problems would be done on a black chalkboard, and I actually liked it, and she was the one to help me be a super math brain with my fast ability in multiplication and division. I wish I could have thanked her for her smart move to build me into loving statistics and using them ever since. I kept sport statistics for the rest of my life, including now.

Two other teachers were Mrs. Logar and Miss Ward. They were both nice and kind and good teachers. They also seemed to have smoked their cigarettes on break and would walk in the room with an un-splendid smell. They were strong, long teachers working with young children.

Yet we always had an exciting spring treat with a delightful, funny professional puppet show. I think that got me interested in puppets, and by fourth grade, I got an old booklet from my great uncle Bob, and the booklet taught all kinds of things about becoming a Ventriloquist.

I would almost always, no always, walk the short walk home for lunch. I had plenty of time to get there as long as I didn't get distracted by the creek or animals or throwing stones in the large cement section from the creeks. Being distracted when I was hungry was not much of a problem, and coming back to school, I wanted time to play. Mom would have a P and J sandwich or some fresh soup, and I would turn on the black-and-white *Bozo the Clown* show at noon.

This was nothing like *it*. Speaking of food…grilled cheese and hot chocolate were a favorite on Sunday nights after church. Yes, I would dunk the Velveeta grilled sandwich in my chocolate milk. I would and still do dunk most sandwiches. Ingie's roast beef with tatas (potatoes), peas, and gravy was a treat meal for our family occasionally.

I liked to stay up until Dad came back from work, and he would bring a delicious Ledo's pizza, one of the best in the Chicago area at that time, and Lockport had an Archie's Pizza that was fantastic and very unique with a taste that was addictive for the hungry, those who need stress relief, want to socialize, or just crave for the afore-mentioned pizza. As a young kid and as an adult, I loved Boza's Hot Dogs, a small place initially for years. Coming through my home-town, my family and I would stop for the sweet diced onion, relish or sliced dill pickle, and mustard for the best hot ever dog! Sister Lori as a little girl, or was it Natalie, didn't want anything on their dogs. That's okay now, but then I would bother anyone just getting a plain hot dog with nothing on it.

Middle School

Many people say that middle school was not a great time of their life or definitely not the best. I am different. So many kids I knew and got to know created a very strong togetherness for the most part. Of course, there were a few who were ignored or teased but only by people who had no compassion and probably had a negative feeling of themselves. There had to be at least two hundred to three hundred middle schoolers at the time, and most but not all were treated with respect.

I felt big going into sixth grade at Kelvin Grove School. Lots of houses full of children, the baby boomers, were surrounded all around the areas, and it seemed all had kids. There were many kids close to the major baseball and football fields and extra yardage to allow more sports. Around the downtown area and across from the Texaco refinery and over by Ludwig School area were more families/kids. My area was between the fire station at Ninth Street and the Grant Store, the cemetery and the houses down to State Street.

So when it came to looking to playing baseball or football away from school, it was not a hard thing to get kids together. I would ride my golden, banana seat bike along with my bat, glove, and hat. Picking teams was the start, and we would play as much as we could. Little League would be going on all summer, and if one was not accepted through tryouts, there was a minor league of teams that provided extra practice to help kids move up in baseball. I played with this league two or three days a week, and it gave me the experience of being on a regular team. I ended up making a team called Savings and Loan Bank.

During the warm/hot summer, we all wore *wool* shirts and pants, hats and big-time shoes with metal cleats, which dehydrated me every game, but that was the same clothing major leaguers wore in the 1960s. I played third base and sometimes shortstop. With all the time I spent throwing rubber balls against our front steps (breaking the glass on the door a few times) and pitching against the neighbor's cement block garage (where I had drawn a small square as a target), I became totally in control of my throws and catches.

I could steal bases and catch most anything hit toward me. However, there were some hard throwing suckers that didn't have the best control of their speed that would scare me a bit when batting, and I would back up and strike out more than I was wanting to do. I was capable though, but there was a day when I was batting against the best pitcher in the league. I was batting against Ricky Ramos who was a great pitcher with a very fast ball and movement, and he also had great control. I hit my only home run of the season on one of his fastballs, with it flying out over the right field fence. Ramos ended up pitching for the Montreal Expos in the Major Baseball Association.

Every year we would have a dinner and trophies and top players, but the best thing was listening to a major league player come and give a speech and sign baseballs for all of us. JC Martin was a good Christian and a catcher for the White Sox for multiple years. My favorite though was Ernie Banks who was the speaker two of the three years I played. I think of him as the greatest ball player in Chicago history, and I was a White Sox fan. The guy was always happy, always willing to talk with anyone, and was known for wanting to play more than one game a day! Wish I wouldn't have lost my two baseballs signed by Ernie Banks and the one by JC Martin.

Another sports-related experience was when I wrote a letter to Bear Bryant the so-called greatest college football coach ever. They hardly lost. I let him know that the Alabama Crimson Tide was my favorite players/team, and I wanted to come down myself and play with the Tide. I also asked him how I could get a 'Bama jacket. Well, he wrote a letter soon and said he was grateful for me loving his team so much. He also pushed me to work hard and never give up, and he hoped to see me when ready to play!

Though I lost some precious childhood sports memorabilia, I have made up with lots. Michael Jordan is signed to a Spalding ball worth much and Koby Bryant with a number 8, and their worth is going up there too. I also have a giant Vince Carter signature and Kevin Garnett photo signed and also the Chicago Bear Dick Butka. I had a basketball signed by the whole Timberwolves team when they were led by Garnett, Wally Szczerbiak, and Cassell...but the signing was slowly fading away.

Back to middle school, there was a day when our teacher had me writing teachers info on the blackboard. There were just a couple guys in the room with me at the time. I had Larry B. sneak up and tickle me under my arm pit that messed up what I was writing. Johnny B. got into the goofing around, and they both came up taking turns to bump my shoulder tickling and ruining the writing. It was funny at first, but I was frustrated finally and told them to stop, but, of course, they had to do it one more time! Behind me again, I had a tap on my shoulder, and I just rammed my right elbow into Larry's belly. But wait...it wasn't Larry or John, it was the superintendent, Mr. Sprague! I freaked! He must have been watching from the hall for a while to see the two guys messing with me. Though I was shocked, he must have understood why I did what I did, and he just gave a small smile with a red face and slowly left the room with Larry and John. I never did get in any trouble. It did end up as the talk of the school that day though.

How about some more junior high sports? Okay, I'll do it anyway. Playing flag football, you had to rip off a colored tag from either side of a player's hip. They had to be on correctly and not hide a flag in a pocket, duh. I don't think I ever saw anyone do that. During my first sixth-grade practice, I was about 4'10" and 85 pounds. Wanting to get an eye by Coach Whalen, I wanted to show him I was a tough guy. So I was racing down the field looking for Jose Medina, who was over 200 pounds and pretty tall and charging down the kickoff. Well, targeting Jose I ran right into him. Hard! It surprised him, but he blew me back a few feet and knocked me out for a few seconds before I was pulled up by the coach who asked if I was okay.

I answered him, "Coach, he is a tough guy to guard, but I am tough too. Don't forget it!"

Coach smiled and answered, "I won't, Dougie, I won't." So it *is* possible for some rough stuff even in flag football. There are no helmets or pads just a school shirt and jeans.

Alvin Green was an All-State basketball player and the quarterback for Fairmont, which was a team that was *always* good in major sports. We only beat them once in three years. We were always good too but usually finished second in our eighth grade school conference. I played a defensive safety and sometimes a running back on offense.

Basketball was always my favorite sport to play and to watch. We had two big guys. Willie Brown was 6'0" as a sixth grader and played the top team in middle school and high school for three years. Our other guy wasn't the best shooter, but he was tall and covered space. Fairmont, again, *always* won the conference and was one of the best teams in the state. Fairmont players were also a major part of the high school Porters and fought in the top ten of Illinois from the 60s through 70s and good teams after that even. Bob Basarich was the coach at Kelvin Grove and finished over many decades at Lockport Central. He also helped produce many All-State players and some All-American Stars also.

In middle school, I played in a tournament at Joliet's St. Patrick, a team that is very good, and has big guys and ability. The end championship was against St. Pat, and we won the championship in a super game my dad and grandpa both watched. Willie Brown was our top star, but multiple of us put in a solid game.

A funny thing was when we were up by eleven points with little time left, Randy came in to play, and he was to throw the ball in after a timeout. He started to freak out because the big guy was all over Randy. So running out of seconds to throw the ball in, he threw the ball right in the face of the St. Patrick star. Laughing was the quick reaction, but the poor guy wasn't happy.

We went to the end of us eighth graders playing in a tournament of eight teams, and many were high-quality schools. The biggest challenge was against Romeoville and, of course, Fairmont. The tourney was divided by rate, and we were number 4 with a record of (26-5), Fairmont number 1 and (28-0) record, Romeoville number 2 (24-2) record. By the end, we were the champions and beat the best and gave Fairmont their only loss, *and* we were so proud and excited it was a diamond in the success!

Middle school was when boys and girls started flirting with each other and having birthday parties. We would have a couple dances at school in the gym every year with music from records kids bring in, and I brought Association songs and Simon and Garfunkel. There would be snacks and juice also. I remember dancing with M. Rapkin with our sweaty hands, and she was a very sweet, friendly girl who had six other siblings in her family I believe. After the dance, I walked her eight blocks to her house, and we held hands the whole way but no kiss, but the next dance, we had a kiss.

D. Finefield was a girlfriend all through eighth grade. We did all the slow dancing at school parties and hugged a lot too until a teacher would pull us away. There was a birthday party at Debbie's house basement, and some of the *pairs* were doing some smooching on a sofa. Phil W. kept intervening with us because he liked Debbie too, but she forced him to go away. Good girl. Our boy/girl relationship ended during the summer, and she ended up going with a big strong guy two years older named Troy McFall, and my older brother David was with his older sister for a while too. Anyway, I ended up friends with them both, and they were married soon after high school.

The Gatlin house across from our elementary school had two sisters close in age, and they would have little parties for drinks and snacks and end up playing spin the bottle. Whoever a girl spun to a boy or boy spun to a girl, they would have to go into a closet and kiss. Sometimes someone would just pretend they were making out. Then after coming out, we would continue taking turns spinning. It was usually four or five girls and same with boys.

The McCarthy family lived just up a few houses from the Gatlins. They had seven kids altogether. We would go over there every once and awhile when parents went out for the night, and Shaun would break out the liquor from multiple bottles and sometimes put water into the bottles afterward if needed. We would take some sips and end up laughing at each other, calling girls on the phone and teasing the four sisters if they were home. Never got in trouble though. Shaun's older brother Pat was a year older, and he actually got mad playing me in tennis by clobbering me with his tennis racket. He was so mad. He got mad easily. Had to watch out for that!

In seventh and eighth grade, a group of us guys would usually tent in the backyard of John Buchanan's house right across of Kelvin Grove. Somebody would sneak down to the local gas station that would be closed and put thirty-five cents in the outside cigarettes machine, and we would be *cool* by lighting one. Some kids at our school would smoke regularly and at recess in a hiding spot. Often someone would bring some cans of beer for each kid. Eventually we would usually move down to a group of girls who were having fun and glad to see most of us. Just talking and laughing, and of course, some would find a corner to kiss. The Grant sisters, Reilly three sisters, Judy and her sister and friends and K. Stash all were very close and would have their own setups and plans.

Kelvin Grove Carnival

The carnival for kids went from 5:00 p.m. to 9:00 p.m. and was a lot of fun. Of course, since I won two trophies, in the last two years for most made free throws out of twenty-five, I just played others for the fun of it and just enjoyed the fun and not fighting to win in that free throw atmosphere. We could buy food with the tickets we bought before the *carnival*. Hot dogs were fifteen cents as well as a Sloppy Joe BBQ. Baked ham was twenty cents with pop and chips a nickel. Sounds like a pretty cheap meal, eh? Ice cream, cake, and pie were ten to fifteen cents.

All the different rooms you needed to use tickets too. Doing the cakewalk would take no more than eight people each walk, and playing music would start with only seven seats. We all would walk carefully around the seats until the music stopped, and kids would yell and rush quickly to find a chair. They would keep playing music until there were only two people left. The winner would get to choose the cake they wanted. There were many, many cakes from parents at home, and this was a fun delicious game.

There was a comic book room, a room for taking photos, one for bowling pins, and one for getting a cheap toy for that, but it was fun. There was also a makeup room, cookie sellers, and an apple tree (don't remember what that was). I won a goldfish once by bouncing a ping pong ball into a small bowl and even brought home two frog pets that lived with me for a year, and then I let in the creek. It wasn't such a big deal for eighth graders, but we were hotshots by then.

Playing basketball was my greatest thing to do. One game as a seventh grader, we were playing Ludwig, and they were not very good. I did my stuff as a point guard by moving and passing the ball and making some cool long shots as did my friends Johnny B. and Timmy the Blond Bomber Boland. At the end of the game, I stepped to talk to N. Dzak who was a short blond cheerleader for Ludwig. At the end of our little talk, I politely asked her if she would like to get together sometime soon. She said *no*. It hurt me a bit for sure, and I felt embarrassed, actually hurt more for a seventh grader.

During our freshman year at Lockport East, a newly built high school for freshmen and sophomores from the baby boomers, we had a fall dance just for our ninth graders, and Nancy asked me if I would go with her as we got to know each other from some classes and student council. I responded with a *no*. I never went to the dance at all, and though we were friends, I have always been sad about my response.

Anyway, besides Nancy, after all of my teammates and I showered and put away our jocks, I took out my delicious, filled up cake with cherries in the middle and top, and whip cream all over the baked cake. I actually won against the rest of culinary class. Many of my basketball players just kind of started grabbing and eating pieces with their hands and gobbled it down! It was really good, and it was very funny at the time until I had to clean up most of the mess of the hallway floor.

Sports

I loved playing sports! School, sports, church, and family were my life. Not necessarily in that order. My older brother Barry was seven years older than me, and for some reason, he still is. So I had a perfect model to follow the same sports that he loved. Actually, basketball was always my favorite to play though Barry played a little. He was a football, wrestling, and baseball player and ended up in the Who's Who book while at Bethel University, for sports *and* academics.

I enjoyed watching brother Bear at his wrestling practice for the LTHS. It was on the pads in the basement with the heat that was always tuned up to sweat people out, make the proper weight on the scale, and build strength and endurance. Coach Zimmer, Mike Zimmer's dad, was a Hall of Fame coach and was in the NFL for a while before sticking in Lockport. Mike played football with me, and he ended up as the Viking's head coach. Anyway, Papa Zimmer allowed Barry to bring me to practice once a week.

There were a couple of black brother monsters that were all state, and they would mess with little sixty-five-pound Dougie for fun. A couple of guys, including Barry, would show me some of the basic moves, that helped me when going to Kelvin Grove Middle School. The Bear worked hard in the heat. I was able to watch all home matches. The Porter gym was like a little Roman Colosseum ring with six-foot brick walls surrounding the court. In his senior year of wrestling, he was one of the wrestlers going to the state finals. Dad and I went to watch and cheer. Mom wouldn't come because she was afraid of him getting hurt, plus taking care of baby Lori.

The first match was in the morning, and he pretty much breezed by many points with almost superpower (remember, I was nine). The second match was much harder. By the third part of the match, he ended with a victory, but he also knocked his left shoulder out of place. It turned out to be a problem. He was so challenging and would never quit, never give up. He had to come back that evening for the chance to go downstate. His coach put his foot under Bear's arm and gave a quick jerk while a slight quick scream responded, but the quick rip put the arm back into place. Over the years, I had to do the same thing a couple of times, and I would flinch at his pain.

He was going against another really good wrestler who knew Bear was damaged goods in the first place. So he went after Barry's weak point right away. My bro would never give up despite the pain. He hung it out all through the match. Squinting often, he worked while in pain, and his left arm was pretty much useless. He lost his opportunity for the State but worked it all out to the end. Strong, very strong, he has always been in life. He actually was working on being against going in the Vietnam draft. A lot of paperwork and defending his religion ended by not passing for his physical and shoulder; no war for him. However, he played football, wrestling, and baseball while at Bethel!

Taft Elementary School in Lockport was close to home. The cool thing about it was a huge tournament in December every year that had all elementary and middle schools jumping to this circus of games. It set things up from fourth to eighth graders. It also had teams based according to weight. Unique. I loved it each year because I was small, light, and very good with the ball. Year after year, I became a little star. This is one where Papa Howie came to watch me often, even Grandpa Sam did a few times. As fourth and fifth graders, we played in a gym that was like playing on a stage. The backboards were huge wooden squares that were a bit different than the regular backboards. The scores were not very high. Usually something like sixteen to nine or up to the twenties. Quarters were shorter in time than the older kids.

Loving basketball as much as I did gave me some confidence because I practiced so much. Dribbling as a 4'5" kid, I could fly around and away with my dribble against any defense. I had the ability to shoot successfully, and my dad and grandpa had a blast watching me play. It made me feel proud. All those games were some of the most enjoyable I ever had in those days. Loving basketball was just a joy for me. Dribbling as a mighty mite around, and I could be a pest defense-wise. I had the ability to shoot successfully inside and outside with quickness.

Playing in the sixth to eighth graders, I became one of the best players because of my weight again. We collected ribbons and trophies every year. I remember getting twenty-eight points in a champion game against Homer Township. I couldn't miss it! The kid who was guarding me ended up being nicknamed Homer T. We became good friends when connecting during freshman high school. It was a weird school because of the huge amount of students, and we went from early morning 'til midday and sophomores from midday 'til early evening, which was the time for sports to practice. Anyway, all those games I played were the most enjoyable and memorable. Good old days.

J. Major had a nice cement hoop set up in front of the house his dad built. We played one-on-one often over about five years. We even played in extreme cold weather, on ice, and/or in the wind. Determined. So we would have on multiple layers of clothes and take off some as we started working hard and get yelled at by his mom. Blocking shots was easier by Jeff, but I got in my share and also got away from his going for a block. We would play games where the first to twenty points wins. Playing as many of those games was our challenge because we even played under an outside light at night. We would play as much as possible, especially from third grade to sixth grade against each other and sometimes a few extra guys.

When the spring weather warmed up, it was time for baseball again. I practiced a lot at the Central School infield, which was filled with large pieces of gravel, and when a ground ball was hit, it was impossible to know exactly where it might hop. This helped me build quick reactions and strengthened my throwing ability. This was fun and good.

Batting was a little bit tougher for me. I had gotten hits and walks and stole bases but struggled some my first two years. My third year was in the Pony League. My biggest thrill was against Rick Ramos again. I ripped a fastball that hit the fence in right field, and I ended up with a triple. I was playing for Crawford Bus now, and all the players were very good, and it ended up being my last official day of baseball. Although, after high school, I played with a team from Lockport, and we were in a Chicago league that was a semipro, of which we were the worst with a record of three wins and nineteen losses. It was just for fun, and I actually won as the pitcher in one game because I threw a pitch where I wound up and threw out my right arm while I threw a *slow* ball from my left hand. That pitch got quite a few strikes and many laughs and "wooos" for the fun.

Wiffle ball games at the T. Boland's yard were a blast in the day. Tim and his brother about four years older, and R. Pilz and other kids our age enjoyed playing for fun but trying hard to win and keeping statistics, especially keeping track of home runs. We would usually have four to five on each team. Using a wiffle ball with holes in it allowed for super big curves! The curve could break like three feet, and it would have to be set properly to be a strike because balls and strikes were used and called for each batter. Often, it was struggling to make a call.

The yard had a fenced outfield I think, and the home runs would be kept on a chalkboard to keep up who had what, and I did pretty well! Multiple blasts were off my skinny yellow bat during the summers. It was a blast! But the league was the most important game.

We would stay with hardball practice and games with our Little League and Pony League. I'd ride my golden banana seat bike up to the field and sweat my butt off. With multiple friends watching the big-time players in the big field after our games, I would watch my brother Barry play in the "major field" with a local team playing teams from different cities. This was when he was home from Bethel. He was a super/tough shortstop, and I remember seeing him hit one out of the deep centerfield one game. I didn't miss any of his games except games away. The boy was my idol. I loved the sports he loved and even loved playing the guitar like he still does.

My Kids

Annika

I broke my finger playing softball freshman year of high school, and I was so mad—mad because I was hurt and mad because I wasn't able to play for a while but even more so mad because the way I got hurt wasn't cool or exciting; it was just weird. I played second base, and I backed up a throw down to the base. The shortstop missed the throw, so I was ready to stop it; and I did, but I stopped it with a finger instead of the glove. It wasn't like I just stuck the wrong hand out or anything; the ball bounced off second base and hit the tip of my middle finger. It was one of the weirdest things that's ever happened to me.

Emilie

Ever since I started playing travel softball, it was typically playing shortstop and occasionally pitching if all other pitchers were tired. However, that's not the case in one tournament when I played with Watertown-Mayer in the summer. We entered the Hutchinson Tournament every year, but this specific year, it conflicted with a few players' personal schedules, leaving us with very few subs. We went about the tournament with several wins, ultimately leading to late in the evening.

A random storm started in Hutchinson soon before our warm-up time for our last game of the day. The umpires kept pushing the start time of the game because of lightning until the storm passed, and a couple more girls left for a vacation. One even quit the team because she didn't get the playing time she wanted! The game ended up starting after 9:00 p.m. We were a team of young, energetic girls, so the time didn't really affect us. However, the field lights weren't very bright, and we only had enough players to fill the field. Where the story really gets tricky is how the girl who left for vacation and the girl who quit randomly were our only catchers.

Our coaches had panicked and randomly chose me to catch. I had never done it before, and I was immediately nervous (which I had never been while playing softball). I stepped up to the task, and we ended up winning. Looking back on the experience reminds me of how sports can impact social and emotional responsibility and develop my self-growth. Stepping into an unknown position and executing tasks that were unfamiliar to me opened several doors of confidence, eagerness, and ambition for new opportunities that I had come my way.

Elijah

Eli was very involved in choirs throughout high school. He had also played leading roles in musicals in elementary school. The choirs he was in at Southwest Christian were solid every year. He was in an a capella group that performed very well at competitions. They also recorded an album, in which he had a solo.

For sports, he tried wrestling early. He struggled, but also was joyful when got a trophy. In baseball, he was the fastest runner. Once as a five-year old, he was so small that when he had on all the catcher's gear, he fell over backwards and couldn't get back up! He also played soccer for a while in elementary school. In middle school, he enjoyed competing in track and field events, such as shotput, discus, and sprints.

A True Worm Story

I am the third of three brothers. My brother Barry was my idol growing up as he was seven years older than me, but he was totally immersed in sports as was I. My brother David, on the other hand, was four years older, and we shared not only the same bedroom but also the same bed for a couple of years. There were complications with this situation back in the day as you might guess. We are very close and loving today but have quite a lot of stories about growing up.

Anyway, we had a couple of acres of land that included an old leaning, somewhat dilapidated garage way in the back across from a graveyard, and we had many different fruit old trees that produced much fruit. There were four different apple trees and two pear trees, a peach tree and two cherry trees—wait, the cherries were in JM's neighbor's yard. Many were destroyed in a tornado, but that is another story. The problem was the youngest brother, me, had to gather all the fallen, rotten fruit that also often had worms.

Well, my brother David pulled out a worm one day and said, "Dougie, would you eat a worm if I dared you?"

I answered, "Why in the world would I eat a worm?"

I was only like five or six years old, and David said again, "I dare you to eat a worm, sissy," and he showed me first to encourage me. I later found out what he really did was slide the worm down as if he were really eating it but dropped it down the side of his mouth. So of course, I picked up another worm and plopped it into my mouth, without chewing, and let the slimy thing go down my throat.

Well then, my brother Dave had to tell my dad about it when he came home from work.

My dad, with a most serious look on his face, asked me, "Dougie, did you really eat a worm?"

I sunk my head down as he stared at me, nodding softly, and whispered, "Ya, Dad, I did, and David tricked me into doing it."

"What do you mean he tricked you?"

I said to Dad, "He really didn't eat his worm but slid it to the ground."

My dad answered, "You know, peanut [my nickname], when we go to church tomorrow, that worm will probably be coming out of your nose, mouth, or ears!"

I was scared. I thought about it all night and went to church the next morning in fear of a worm coming out of my head somewhere. When we arrived at church, my dad and two brothers sat in a pew toward the front where my mom played the piano. I kept checking my nose, ears, and mouth, picturing in my mind what people would think. After checking for about the fifth time, I looked across the pew and saw my dad with a red face. Brother Barry had to get up and leave cause he was laughing quietly but about ready to bust and lose it. David, of course, had a sly smirk, and I knew something was wrong.

I was only a little kid, but I finally realized that the joke was on me. My dad put his arm around me and said, "Don't worry, chief [another nickname], there won't be a worm coming out. It was just a prank pulled by your brother."

Needless to say, I never ate a worm again. However, I did pull the same trick four years later on little sister Lori!

High School

It was exciting to be ready to go to a high school. A new school was built to bring in freshmen and sophomores from ten to twelve middle schools. We were in the middle of the baby boomers! There were more students at each level, and even though it was a new place for learning, it still had to change things around. Freshmen would be in school from 6:30 a.m. to 11:30 a.m. and the sophomores 12:30 p.m. to 5:30 p.m. That was an awful beginning for me going to a new building and a nasty time separated from sports in a rotten way.

Before school started, we had to use a map to find what classes we had and where they were in the school, plus exposure to each person we would work around and pick up our books. It was great to see old friends around and new possible friends that we played sports against. I rode my golden, banana seat, high-backed bar for support straight up Seventh Street to the thrilling, exciting, and a bit frightening spot with so many people.

Some were friendly, some ignored me, and some hugged me. Lots of pretty girls. Many students were strangers, and many would become friends with me. But it settled down after getting to know a teacher or two, finding out what time each class would be, the number on each door, handing out a syllabus, and lastly checking out the beautiful gyms and huge lunch room.

Bringing things outside after talking and watching all that was around, I went to get my stuff in my backpack, ready to ride home and felt thankful that the whole process of the day was over. However, my golden, banana seat bike had been stolen, and I never got it back. I never had a bike after this one. It took me all over Lockport for a few years and was a sad loss. Great way to start a new voyage in my education.

I did sign up to play football. Our coach was a huge, muscled dude who played for Purdue. Our coach was a good guy and a tough guy and a player's guy. The only problem was that we all were in school at 6:30 a.m., and football practice was from 6:00 p.m. to 7:30 p.m. Not a well plan set up, but I went in on day one and picked up my multiple pads, practice uniform, helmet, spike shoes, and new jock…and the practice began. Being late August and after only playing flag football in those days it was much more of a challenge to practice in the heat.

Time spent every day was tiresome with such an early wake-up with Mom driving me off, especially since my bike was gone. I felt bad that I wouldn't let her kiss me goodbye or let her hug me. I would quietly, at 6:23 a.m., get out of the car. Then I would get rides to and from practice in the evening because Dad was at work, and Mom had two young girls to watch. I did use practice to help burn out my frustration when physical football had me practicing as a defensive back looking for tackles and even more for interceptions. But I only ended up with 1 or 2 interceptions, 1 fumble recovery and one black eye on the very first kickoff of the first game. I went after a huge guy, just like in Middle School, and got pats on the back, again, for going at it. But this was all over after our 6 games, but it was cool.

I didn't play in my second year of football. More on friends and girls and parties and the use of weed and the fact that the school learning was not working for me with the late-evening practices. I did stay with the student council for the second year. I would only get good grades on things I liked. I was kind of like my son Eli in high school, but he didn't make the big mistakes I did. Hope he stays away from what I went through…for sure. I would only do well in the classes I liked. Mrs. Walker, who also had my brother Barry, was a great literature teacher. German was a bit cool at first but continuing and gaining more depth went from a B to a D by my second year. I certainly remember enough of German to be married to a lady with a German background! My Swedish grandpas would roll in their graves if they knew who I married since they were both related to WWI. Actually, my grandpas would love my wife as they were loving, Christian men for sure.

Freshman Earth Science was fine, and I sat with a cool girl named Charma T., and we would laugh and tease each other while getting ready for class. After weeks of getting along, I asked her if she would meet me at the school's dance. The year 1969 was not the period where white and black people were getting together in dances. There were a lot of racial problems at the time. Martin Luther King Jr. was one who when killed had the country at war because of the unfair treatment of a human group of mostly good families. There were looks from other people of all colors that we would be doing the wrong thing. We stayed friends in class but realized that going any further would cause trouble. Our school was to the point that the black students and white students even had their own dances. Sad, it was soon after Charma and I talked about a dance. Maybe that cut to separate dances, but there were stronger problems going on.

The second year of school was biology, and I hated it. I loved it in college, but I was not connected with this teacher. Thus, my C/D grades were given. German stayed in the Ds, and my language and literary classes were great. I put up with Coach Bill Zimmer and Mike and worked hard in wrestling. I had great strength, but I needed to build strong moves depending on different situations. Monroe was a really good wrestler and a year older than me, and the reason was for me to build my clever moves and strength. Ended up that I finally beat him in practice, and he was a top wrestler on the senior team. I didn't go back as a junior.

Of course, as my connection to *hippies*, like friends and partiers, I dropped after my sophomore winter. Drugs were easy to get and hanging with others and testing different drugs are demonic in my thoughts. What better way for evil to take over kids and build them to nowhere and often death? So many hell-bound traps can put a person on the wrong road.

I did play golf under Coach Bob Basarich, who was well known for all the great basketball teams and for the many years he was there at the *pit*. We would practice/play at the nine-hole Texaco course, which is still there. I used Barry's old wooden putter which was cool, and the rest of his clubs were okay for a starter.

In the last two years of school, I graduated in early January, and I was keeping track of basketball rebounds, free throws, where shots were taken, what they made, and what they didn't, and steals, blocks, and fouls. It was the kind of stuff I still do at home. I loved helping out a great team. The best part was going to the Pontiac Tournaments every December with school out and the state finals in Champaign, Illinois. I went to almost all of them and did stats for most.

Trips after High School

Things were getting lost in my life. I graduated from high school in early January by getting enough classes done by doing a night class putting on a mask and learning about welding metal. Thinking back, I even had a bad dream that I really didn't do enough to pass that class and didn't really graduate. I tried some junior college and did well but backed away from it mainly because I didn't have a car and those who I got rides with had weed to smoke on the way to class. Didn't work for me.

I hitched a ride with John "Crazy Fool" Liker. We were going to see friends in Colorado, but we got no farther than the border of Iowa and there was a blizzard and I-80 was shutting down. Before it totally shut down, we were on the road anyway, hoping for help. Two guys in a large van stopped to carry us which actually would help them put weight in the empty van. They were from the University of Nebraska and had dropped off a piano in Illinois so they were thankful that we could help control the van in the blizzard even though we went about twenty miles an hour and often started to go sideways.

It took a long time to Nebraska, and at about 2:00 a.m., when we got to their university apartment, they felt bad for us. We slept in their place and the girlfriends of the two guys made us breakfast at about 10:00 a.m. Then they dropped us off on I-80, and we continued toward Manitou Springs, Colorado to visit a few friends (four to six) from Lockport. We finally made it, and the weather was pretty good, especially compared to what we went through to get there. Speaking of spring, I got some fizz tablets and threw them in the spring water taken from a fountain, but I didn't know it was natural soda water. It was terrible! I did not drink any more of the taste.

So we were staying with the Borman brothers at a large old cabin where it was quite a ways up Pike's Peak. It was a good time to hang out with the brothers. The girls were S. Shedowski and Susan. Both girls were living at the cabin with two older guys from *home*. I'll just say it was a happy, hippie atmosphere.

A cool thing is that George's girlfriend was Kathy Peters who was the daughter of "Mr. Clean!" He was the real live one on the TV commercials for the "all-purpose liquid cleaner." We met the dad who was actually House Peters Jr. He died in 2008 at the age of ninety-two. However, he did more than just famous commercials. Roy Rogers, Gene Autry, and *Perry Mason* were all famous in the 1950s, 1960s, and into the 70s. Peters was a part of movies with all the famous people above as well as the *Twilight Zone*.

After that delightful time and hanging around the mountain and city, we hiked up about seventy miles to Denver and hung with another Lockport guy who was going to school. He was more than a groomer but trained as a farrier and capable of shoeing all types of equine feet, whether normal or defective, making shoes to suit all types of work and working conditions, and devising corrective measures to compensate for faulty limb action. Don't ask me about it all though. He was going back to Lockport, and we had our ride to end the trip. I cannot remember his name! He was a friend of Bruce and George though.

Another trip between when I was nineteen years old, Tom K. and Fast Eddie went together in Tom's old truck to visit G. Goodlander at his college. It was a unique experience that I mostly enjoyed. It was a long trip down, of course. Hanging out at the school and getting to know multiple people besides Gary was fun, and some serious conversations made it better.

There was a very cool quarry close by, and it was decided that many people agreed to go swimming. I am not a very good swimmer, but the cool water in the hot sun was good enough for me. Before leaving, we all were passing out special mushrooms, which I had never had before. Reaching the quarry water, multiple people were swimming across to the other side. Since everyone did it, I took off myself and was a little way behind Tommy K. I was about twelve feet away from shore in very deep water. I struggled and went down once and popped back up, but I was weak. Tommy saw I was in trouble, and as I went down again, he pulled me up and dragged me to the close shore.

I didn't even think of swimming back, so I walked all around the large quarry. As I walked, I thought of how close I was to losing it. Coming back to the college party, I was freaked out still and had multiple people talking to me about almost drowning. It was a tough adventure, and I waited quietly until we moved out from Texas.

The three of us in Tom's *old* truck were to meet Willie and Judy in Montello, Nevada. Believe it or not, they were on their *honeymoon*! Thinking back, it seemed a very goofy/strange action moving into their hotel room, three of us, and we visited the Million Dollar Cowboy Bar. Hanging around the saddled seats with the newlyweds for an hour or so. After another day the three of us were off in the *old* truck headed for home.

Unfortunately, the truck started messing up. It kept going into neutral and it was a struggle to get it back into gear. We stopped multiple times to try and fix the problem, but it only got worse. On the last 150 miles, we couldn't get any faster than 20–35 mph as the stick would stay stuck in second gear. But at least we made it and were exhausted out of the last drive for sure.

Another trip was with John, and we were planning to go up to St. Paul and hang out with Brother Barry. We headed up to Rockford on the first day of the trip. Eventually, a guy picked us up as he was going to Rockford. Getting there he said he was going to the same hotel that we wanted to stay because it was cheap. He offered to take us out for dinner and to a bar. It was obvious he was gay and kind of scary. So we did *not* go with him at all. As a matter of fact, we blocked the door with a chair under the door handle and put a dresser behind that. We were paranoid because it wasn't a very good hotel or a very safe-looking area. But I remember well that I sat and wrote a couple of songs about our traveling on napkins and signed them "Bob Dylan." I left the napkins and we decided to hitch back the one hundred miles to Lockport.

The coolest vacation was with Eddie and his new green Volkswagen. It was Tom, RR, and myself with a smashed amount of needed things on the roof and hood. Grand Canyon here we come! No problem with his new car. I was not used to a stick shift car so I struggled a bit when I was driving to give Eddie a break. We stopped in a high area of the mountain that had a herd of bison fenced in not far from where we were tented.

So we decided to go to the fence in the dark, jump over the fence, and start walking out in the field. After we had been walking for a while, all of a sudden we heard the rumbling of the bison herd. It got louder and louder to the point that the ground started to rumble, and we all took off as fast as we could to get away! After getting back from the adrenaline we kinda figured out that they were actually running away from us...I think.

Going to the Grand Canyon for the next few days, we tented up and decided to walk down a couple of miles to get to the bottom of the canyon. We each had a water can, but it was in the upper 90s, and I drank mine on the way down. Ed and Tom wanted to stay down and chill out, but I decided to go right back up. (Duh!) Halfway up, a Japanese lady saw I was struggling and dehydrating, and she offered me her canteen. Taking a big swig, I realized it was some kind of wine. I just started feeling even worse. Getting three-fourths way up, I began to throw up.

I finally made it to the top and puked some more, and I went straight to the hot tent where I finally had some water and laid down on my bag. The boys eventually came back up and were fine and realized I was sick as I explained my wonderful climb.

The next morning, after drinking mucho water, we were on our way to a lake close by to swim and cool off. A few girls asked us to join them at the lake, and we hung out with them for a while. They were nice kids, and we had fun before leaving with a "thank you for the company." We left the next morning, and the trip was overall a great time! Thanks, Eddie!

My final traveling, post-high school, in my eighteen to twenty life experiences, was going to the Sedalia, Missouri Rock Festival in the middle of the woods. We got there early the afternoon before it began on July 19 through the twenty-first. We all had tickets, but many people started busting in freely, and there were at least 250,000 thousand people. Glad we were early for tenting and a good position for musicians performing. It was actually bigger than Woodstock some say! We also watched the second day, cars lined up for about seventeen miles, according to estimates, just to get on the land.

My clothes were deer skin moccasins I bought up in Cook, Minnesota, and an Uncle Sam red-white-and-blue top hat, and I had a colorful beaded necklace around my neck from a tribe in south Colorado. Along with that was no shirt because of the heat. What a hippie look in the early 1970s, eh?

The music was fantastic. There were at least seventy bands. We got way up front below the performing acts the first day and night. Ted Nugent and his band played at midnight the first day, and we were right under the stage. It got so crazy that I was actually crunched to the point that both my feet were off the ground from people continuing to press into a two-hour high-blast performance from midnight to 2:00 a.m.! He didn't want to stop.

Again it was over 250,000 people! There were plenty of multiple drugs being sold and being given away. There were also weird tents of women waiting for anyone to come in, and the lines were very long to have sex. I could not pay attention to the whole idea myself as it seemed pretty weird. I wasn't that far from the history of my Christianity. I was at the time getting far away from my faith, but there was always a light in my life that kept me in safety regardless of my understanding. The drugs allow unseen demonic trapping looking for destruction.

By the end of the festival, there were an extreme amount of people that died because of a mixture of drugs and lack of water stopped for hydration. The music was great, and the ability for us all to be okay and make it home was a blessing. One strange piece of information I found many, many years later (2020) was that a woman who worked at MNCS as a para and at the cafeteria was at the same crazy festival. It is a small world!

The best music for me was: Eagles, America, Bruce Springsteen, Ted Nugent, Joe Walsh, REO Speedwagon, Jeff Beck, Blue Oyster

Cult, Nitty Gritty Dirt Band, Boz Skaggs, Marshall Tucker Band, Amboy Dukes, and about fifty-nine more bands. If you don't know most of them, google it and see what you think.

Coming back from Sedalia, Missouri, I went searching for multiple jobs...A friend of mine helped me get a job working on the nearby canal barges that needed to be cleaned up. My initial barge had come up from New Orleans, and it wasn't bad to do cleaning, but it was quite a bit of work. We had to learn about the lowering of water that also needed to be balanced according to how much weight was on the barge. We saw a couple of stingrays flopping in the dirty water of the spillage. Kind of cool. What wasn't cool was rats running off and hiding as quickly as possible and me having to clean up their crap and put dead rats in a bag. This was usual of barges with wheat or corn. I only lasted about a week and a half but got decent money for the work.

I ended next working for a friend's dad in Lockport, and we had different custodial jobs by cleaning offices and doing basic things like vacuuming, washing windows, cleaning desks, bathrooms, kitchens, and cigarette dishes. What I actually enjoyed was stripping wood and tile floors and replacing it with new wax and buffing them afterward after they were sealed. Also, I remember working with a few other friends at an animal hospital that had an open room needing cleaning but also openly having medication for animals and easy to take. One of the other janitors was an animal himself, who took multiple pills used for sedating animals before an operation to prevent pain. Unfortunately, we all got kicked out.

I needed a different way of living but was unsure what would work. The parties and drugs were not doing any help in going back to my faith. My parents were arguing often, and I remember sitting at the top of our winding steps listening to them argue. It made me feel sadly for sure and hurt and thought that maybe I was a part of the problem.

So I got some money and went to St. Paul on a bus and moved into the same house as my brother Barry and we had separate rooms upstairs. In between our rooms, we had a small frig for food and drinks. I didn't have a car and usually couldn't ride with Barry because he worked full-time. So I got little jobs that would be a few days by bus or brother's car.

Another job was moving all kinds of junk from an old house and cleaning was done with one other guy. We were getting it ready for new things that would be put in when it was completed. After the first day of work, I received my first cash for a modest amount for seven hours of work. The owner asked if we would like to go to a nearby bar, and have some food and a few drinks, but I didn't want to go, I wanted to go *home*. My cleaning buddy did the same. The next day after work, the owner paid us both again and asked us about the bar and food again. We looked at each other and agreed to give it a try.

Now the owner seemed to be on the side of a gay guy, but I didn't want to ask him about my thought of him being gay, and I didn't want to hurt his feelings if he wasn't gay. Right away there was a huge lady coming up to us to ask what we wanted to drink.

She asked me in a very low voice saying, "So what do you want cutie?"

I took a beer, and by looking around, I could see easily this was a gay/transgender bar. My working partner also agreed to get away before it was to be troubled at all. Neither one of us came back to work again even though we both needed cash, but at least we made some. I lived close enough to walk back *home* after stopping at a bookstore on Snelling Street, and it is still there.

Barry got a kick out of my story and said St. Paul has many gays and said, "You should keep an eye on the people you pass." So we ate some super Swedish bread from Grandma Swanson and some of Eva's summer sausage too. On the next night, I had more of the bread with my liver sausage and Grandma's homemade canned sweet pickles. The best supper!

Another job I had was at a Jewish home for the elders. It was just a short walk to get there so I didn't have to worry about the weather or worry about buses or the need for a car. It was part-time, and I earned a low hourly salary, but working with some old people at mealtime was okay, but I couldn't take the smell of *cleaning* and giving old Jewish men baths.

Inside my soul, it just didn't seem to be the right place. I did enjoy going out with Barry and his friends and parties and did not want to go back to Lockport mainly because of the death of a good friend and a bad atmosphere with Mom and Dad. I certainly didn't want to leave Barry. It wasn't easy to do.

Lost Friends in the Past

I don't like getting into much detail with some history, being in a stage of fantasy and living with just a distant light of God. I had a very close friend who was killed while arguing with another car driver late at night on the hill of a country road stopped and facing each other. Both cars had lights on shining brightly both ways.

A car was coming fast toward my friend's car, and the bright lights must have blinded the guys standing on the road. JL was smacked hard, and an ambulance brought him to St. Joseph Hospital as fast as possible. A couple of us were in the hospital and saw him in bad shape with an ear ripped out and his face half gone. It didn't take long before he was a twenty-year-old dead friend.

His name was Crazy Fool, and it was the truth. He was a good high school football linebacker and an even better long runner in track. He lived in an old house on Ninth Street with his granny who was a bit crazy herself. Lots of *crazy* parties went on in that house with many people. He would also talk with me about Jesus every once in a while.

I wrote a song for John in my room about him before his funeral. I played the song for his parents and sisters, and they appreciated it. The casket was a closed one, which made sense, but I did get the chance to drop my song with him. When our friends were taking the casket out, it was a hard thing for me and all of us to go through. It hurt a lot and took a long time to chill out.

Bradley C. lived close to where I stayed and often hung out with Brad and his two younger brothers. He struggled with self-confidence I think and was taken up by unseen powers that did nothing but destroy. I was in the same trouble, but because I was surrounded by many family Christians, especially grandparents, I eventually started to come closer to Jesus. All of a sudden, Bradley came out of the bar that is filled with drunks and druggies as usual and walked out the door and went close by train tracks late at night. He laid down on a track and was found early the next morning ripped apart.

Another good friend from Kelvin Grove and High School and beyond. Russ was a very intelligent brain but too attached to the hard drugs that took control of his life. This stuff was back in the late 1960s and 1970s drugs of any kind could be sold right off the streets until police started building a better attack. You never knew exactly what mixture could be in the stuff. This poor, sad young friend went to the highway above the canal and homes, and he jumped off. I am sure it was too much brain and soul attacker, and it makes me sick of the evil spiritual war in this world. He died young.

PK was a strong leader of the group of many tight friends. He lived longer than others but was still very young. He played basketball for the Porters of Lockport, and after high school, we had a team that played in our upper teens and early 20s. We played with some of the older guys and had like eight teams that was nothing but fun as everyone knew everyone.

PK started working construction work and made good money and worked hard and played hard. He liked his beer. He also early on was able to afford a hot engine gray Nova that he loved to fly around with friends. He also had a Honda Cruiser that he was crazy with sometimes. I remember when I rode behind him as he was swiveling back and forth until *we* crashed and rumbled on the asphalt. We survived of course but I had no helmet. Might make sense to this day perhaps?

PK would share with any and all friends until at the age of twenty-nine had a serious brain aneurysm, and he passed away. I was so hurt by previous deaths I couldn't handle going to his funeral. I started not going out with the many friends left.

Gerry, my first Cuz, played in the park service basketball too and we gave his team a challenge even though his guys were two to three years older. I would hang out at Gerry and Patty's little house on Hamilton Street quite often. They married when they were both like nineteen and eighteen, and Patty had a baby "right away," and his name is Michael. Gerry is still alive, praise God, but I am praying for him and the kids to find time for salvation.

Patty had a second baby boy, and his name is Erik, and his family is saved and has been for a long time. Patty started working in the Kelvin Grove cafeteria when their boys started school and kept on working there even though the boys were out of school. Probably something like twenty years working would be my guess. Mark was Patty's younger brother, and Mark was a year older than me, but he was on our park service b-ball team too. He also played through Little League and Pony League, and I played against his teams often over the years. He was a hard-throwing left-hander who wasn't always accurate. It freaked me out to try to hit against him. Pitches by my head, behind my back, and just fastballs, I stepped back even though I didn't need to do it.

After we grew up, he got himself into the Lockport Police Station, and after a few years, he ended up in the State Police or the Will County Police—not sure. I didn't see him much for a couple of years, and it came to the point where it seems he had taken too much to handle with all the crap he must have seen. He passed away himself at an early life, and it surprised everyone, especially his wife and his sister Patty, Gerry, and the whole family and friends.

Gerry has his two sons and their families but lives by himself, though, I am sure he has old friends hanging out with him. Patty ended passed away after battling a long illness until 2017. Everyone loved being with her. I need to talk with Jerry as it has been a long time, but I do pray regularly.

My oldest friend who has been mentioned in my *book* earlier was/is J. Berglund. My family got to hang out in his house in deep southern Illinois. The kids were thrilled, I think, with his pond where he raises catfish and passes dog food on the water, and they would shoot up in a second. There were many very large ones, and he said he would eat one every once in a while and keep a strong amount.

My kids and Karen were unable to know JB's wife as she passed away thirty-plus years ago I think. She was having problems that the hospital checked and said it was not serious. Three times JB brought her in because she was getting worse and worse. The third time in the hospital it was too late. She passed away at an early age for sure!

JB always struggled with Jesus even though he was in a solid Christian family. He just got too far in dealing with the cocaine. I am sure he has struggled with the loss of his wife. She was a wild one too, but she did come to a time where she was going to church. I hope she is in heaven as she was a good friend of mine too.

In JB's early life and we were both like sixteen, his sister Lynn passed away. She always had a cut-off leg since I knew her, and she handled it well for years, but in the late 1960s, she passed away. She was a very sweet person, but it must have been as much of a pain to JB as me losing a brother. A brother who is still alive but hiding in his own world.

Army

Getting back to Lockport when Mom and Dad were separated after twenty-nine years of marriage, they were in the process of divorce. Natalie was only about eleven years old and would move in with Ingie and her new husband Dean who had four children in his family. Having Natalie go through leaving her friends in Lockport and being unknown to the children of Dean's family and away from Lori and myself (as David and Barry were already gone), she had to be mentally and safe-wise confused and sad as we all were. She also had to go to a school where she knew no one but her unknown half-sister at the time.

The rest of our Anderson family were deeply hurt also (check my dad's song). Lori and Barry were married soon, and David was just back from Vietnam, Cambodia, and Thailand during the war. Barry broke his marriage with Ginny at Bethel who later married Barry's best friend. It was soon after that Arthur and Eva both passed away. Eva and Barry were very close, and this all together created a strong tension war within his mind, soul, and heart.

I signed up for the army before the divorce and let Mom know where I was going. She cried and cried sitting on our old bright-blue sofa for quite a while drying her tears on my cheek and shirt. She thought it was her fault for my decision. It wasn't. My dad thought I was making a good choice and was proud of me. Grandpa Sam was in the army during WWI in France, Dad was in Japan after WWII, David was in the air force in Vietnam War, and here I was going to the army. Pop took me to the Joliet Greyhound bus stop to bring me to "Lost in the Woods" Missouri for boot camp the next morning.

My dad actually showed me a couple of pictures in Japan at the very end of the war. He gave me a picture of a Japanese young man in the middle of where he was going. It would be about another four miles. Papa stopped in his jeep and brought the young man because this Japanese man had no legs. They were blown off in war, and he now was moving with his hands under his waist. My dad left a note that read, "If I ever am having a bad time or I am struggling, I will think back to the legless smiling Japanese young man in my jeep!" Pop also gave him a chunk of cash.

I felt I needed to build strength, get my act together, and trust Jesus to be right by my side. I had to believe my choice was the hope and choice of Jesus. I needed to build confidence and control of negative situations. It was a strange trip, especially when I changed the ride to a military bus. When arriving at Fort Leonard Wood, we had time to sleep late in the morning and went out through the process of getting our military clothes, going in for our thick black glasses, boots that hopefully fit, hats, the process of going to meals and information on being a strict soldier ready to work hard over the next twelve weeks. I also had to take a blood test and urine test for any drugs. I did, and it happened *not* to be marijuana or other hard drugs but pills I snuck out of my nurse mom's dresser!

Then after getting the initial information, came buzzing off my hair completely, and the beginning of marching, saluting, and repeating lyrics as we stayed orderly stepwise. One old chant was, "A yellow bird, with a yellow bill, was sitting on, my window sill, I lured him in, with bits of bread, and then I smashed his blank head!" Left, left, left, right…

Practicing basic first aid was learning CPR and practicing on a partner without actually doing mouth-to-mouth—Thank goodness! Using the arm sling is for the majority of arm and upper limb injuries. The elevation sling can be used to elevate fingers, for example after a crush injury. Bandaging a bleeding arm or leg was another basic aid skill taught.

Working time in boot camp was from 5:00 a.m. when the drill sergeant would walk in where the mucho bunks were lined next to each other with wooden boxes at the end of our beds for clothes.

Then when hearing a *loud* voice, we would have to immediately get up, put on clothes and boots, and fix our beds perfectly, or you'd be doing push-ups.

Next, we would go outside and line up at attention and then spread out to do many push-ups and jumping jacks and then run a couple of miles. Coming back we would line up, go across monkey bars that were very thick around and roll loosely making it difficult for anyone with smaller hands...like me! I would rarely ever make it through without cutting a hand with a fingernail from slipping away from the rolling bar!

Troops would be at ease in line as one by one would go into the breakfast room, waiting to get some food. The food was okay, but we had to eat fast if late in line. Plus, I always have been a slow eater, so I changed just for boot camp. There was a class for our M16 rifle. We had to pass the ability to take all the parts off and put them all together in what seemed impossible for passing in such few seconds. But they knew what they were doing as teachers, and I passed without a problem (unlike the bars).

Obstacle courses were crawling small tunnels, moving on the ground with my weapon under wires and sometimes in muddy water. After practicing this through the days we would be tested by crawling low, with weapons, and under live fire for fifty yards. One must pass it like everything else we do. Other things we would do are walk/run on logs and climb various walls of wood.

After we had taken apart our rifle and put it back again, we were happily ready to go to a shooting range and shoot live. You must hit twenty-three to twenty-nine out of the forty targets to earn that qualification. If you do a little better (thirty to thirty-five), you qualify for the sharpshooter badge. To get an expert badge, you must hit at least thirty-six targets. I was a sharpshooter. We were taught and practiced shooting laying down, standing up, from a fox hole, and off on one knee. Drill Sergeants were very strict and orderly where a safe distance line took turns with one person waiting behind the shooter and the others further behind in lines. Checking my hits and improving in weeks, shooting there was fun!

Bivouac was pretty cool. We had basic small tents without a floor made for two people. I say no floor because my partner and I realized we were in the area of copperhead snakes...lots of baby copperheads! So we decided to move away, far away, and try to sleep that first night. We had to use a compass to specific places and move to the next to bring us back where we started. Another passed the test.

Before throwing any grenades, we had to practice a specific form with one knee in front of you and back leg straight back, one arm straight out front and the back hand holding the grenade. Then pull out pin, throw the grenade straight ahead where the front hand is pointing and off it goes to your target. This would be done standing also.

Coming to boom, boom time for this to pass was very exciting and anxious to get my turns. We had a target to hit with our throws and sparks would fly all over the place along with dirt and rocks. We went on to learning about M2 50 Cal and M60 machine guns. It uses full-power rifle rounds and weighs 23 pounds. Both the M2 and M60 have cyclic rates of 550 rounds per minute. A lot of power to feel those shots going on.

The coolest one was firing an anti-tank rocket launcher. If caught behind the launcher, you would catch a blow of fire. The same amount of power going forward comes out of the back also. What was interesting is that it didn't go anywhere as quickly as launchers can go today.

After working on a tactical march, we reached realistic war training that was hard working days toward the end of the boot. Working days were from 5:00 a.m. to 10:00 p.m. and getting two hours of watch twice a week. It could wear you down mentally and physically, and that is another test.

We also had to succeed on a confidence course that had all kinds of wood-built challenges, and two, I remember were a forty-foot and sixty-foot climb that you had to pull yourself up step by step with seven or twelve steps that required being pulled up for some.

Oh, I almost forgot that we all had to take turns in small groups going into a small one-room structure and had a wonderful experience to go through. We were taught how to put on properly, our gas mask, and be sure it was closed tight. As we went in the little building, we would be told when to put on our masks with gas all over the place. Then just to get an example, each person had to take the mask off and not leave until you breathed in the gas. The more you *hold* your breath, the worse the breathing in gas would be. People were tearing up like crazy, snot would be flowing out of their noses, and some were throwing up and yelling. I didn't wait to do my breathing, and it was not enjoyable, but I made it through without being nailed too badly at all.

The PT was the last test. One was to run a mile in less than eight minutes. Not a big deal. I ran the first three laps with Christian, a super four-minute runner, and friend from Jamaica. In the fourth lap, I had to walk most of it because I overdid staying with Christian, but I still came in with four minutes in the first three laps and three and a half minutes in the last lap. There were also a couple of exercise pieces that were easy. My fear was the stinking monkey bars! Well, the testing on the bars *did not* end up being a big deal! The bars were smaller, and they were closer together! I flew through the bars faster than anyone! Anyone except Charlie.

We had our graduation out on the marching field, and there were a decent amount of parents, not mine. Stiff, proud pacing, saluting properly, and happy to be successful in this step, which I looked forward to the future.

Friends Come Fast When Stuffed Together for 12 Weeks

Gary Berry and David Brakebill were friends who followed me to Fort Sam Houston. K. Rock was short like me and from Milwaukee. We both got together well, and we both had funny things to talk about. We ended up in the last days of boot camp as being Rock and Roll. He was tough as a *rock*, and I was a bit chubby, although I was in solid health by the end day. We both loved music and would sing along to please the multiple soldiers in our group. We also went to church and sang in there too. Mike Cunningham was an eighteen-year-old who was always happy and liked to play me in a pool table when we had the chance at the military bar. L. Tikka was my partner in Combat Medic classes. L. Hatta was a Japanese little guy about 5'3" who lived in Hawaii. He was hilarious, and I enjoyed the time with him. He was a tougher guy than you would think. P. Brooks was a big, happy dude who had a much older brother, Larry Brooks, who was a top defensive lineman playing for the Los Angeles Rams.

The next day everyone was given their pass as to where they would be going next. Two buddies of mine from boot camp were close friends while we were together. They both were from Arkansas and would be riding the bus to Fort Sam Houston along with the well-known Brooke Army Hospital. It was a peaceful ride, and we were all excited to make the step up as combat medics and/or clinical specialists.

We were assigned a large open, second-floor section of bedding, and I chose the top bed in my area, which had plenty of air-conditioning, which was great because walking out of the building would start the sweat immediately, especially in the summer. I also hid unallowed material above, in the ceiling. I played a lot of pool and made a little money playing. I also ran into Alan who was a friend from high school, and he was a drug lover, and we were both freaked out that the other was in the military. He was close to graduating and going to Hawaii for his military assignment. One I am sure he was pushing for it initially.

Our drill sergeant wasn't a driller at all but was a twenty-year soldier with plenty of wartime and had solid explanations instead of forcing us. I appreciated him quite a bit. We were mostly pretty much on our own after some early workouts and multiple classes as medics-to-be. My two boot buddies were in a different medic station, but we would get together usually in the evenings and on weekends.

Classes were fine and interesting as we were being taught similar to paramedics except we were preparing to be combat medics, first responders, being thrown to be the first responders dealing with straightening out triage injuries as well as illnesses and saving lives on-site problems. We also practiced giving shots to people by using oranges as a similar feeling to human skin when injected. After practicing and understanding the process, we would be with a partner to try it with each other. The same thing was learned and practiced when we worked on drawing blood.

My partner was a nice kid I knew from boot camp and when he was *ready* to draw blood from me, I said, "Ahhh, no, not yet!"

The reason for that was he was shaking with the needle like crazy and I didn't want to be ripped, in or by my vein until he could chill out. So he went at me again and it wasn't much safer but he made it through. Hallelujah! I was pretty nervous too to draw his blood, but I did okay on the first try. Other classes we went through were practicing how to sterilize surgical equipment, CPR practice, and things like patient care technology. There were specific medicines that we went through and how each med was used. Clinical classes were the last before it was time to go home.

What was nice about Fort Sam Houston was we had time off during all evenings and weekends. Just hanging out, relaxing, goofing around, and talking about the future. I went to church on Sundays.

My two buddies and I went off the fort multiple times during the weekends. We went to San Antonio a few times. The Alamo was kind of cool to check out the history…and it was free. The Riverwalk was cooler from the extreme heat and sweating from humidity and just a relaxing walk along the river. Yes, we stopped at the Pearl Brewery, but there wasn't any beer there.

The San Antonio Zoo was a great place to go. We went there one night at the zoo when there was all kinds of music and entertainment and checking out the animals, as well as girls (this was way before Karen came along). There were vendors walking around selling foods and beers. They had a great setup for the park and a solid amount of background to the water animals, big cats, and many other parts for a good vision of the animals. It was soon after the zoo again when I was able to fly home and get to be there for David and Robin's wedding. That was great for sure, and I was proud to be there for Bro David. Also, I had time to go to the beach with family in Indiana before I flew back to Texas.

Illinois National Guard

Coming back *home* was at that time when my dad moved. It was recently David's apartment in Joliet before he was married and moved in with his wife Robin in New Lenox with a daughter, Caris, who was very young at that time. So it really wasn't home where I was now, and it was strange. Mom was married to Dean now and they had an old house that was around east Joliet. 524 East Seventh in Lockport was no longer a part of my life.

Also, I was home for one week when I had to prepare to get more army clothes, helmet, gas mask, boots, and a cap to be ready to go up to Fort McCoy in Wisconsin for ten days, and I was the new medic in the group which meant I needed to get the hardest jobs and prove myself.

The first days at Camp 1 and 2

Meeting all the medics and higher-level medical guys, one of them ended up being a friend of my brother Barry and who played high school football with him also. That was a cool person who was there, to begin with. Another Lockport person, Gryzetch, was a paramedic at the Lockport Firehouse, which was only a couple blocks up from where my siblings and I grew up, except for Natalie who moved away with my mom when the divorce was settled. Gary Lemke was a quick friend as he came in the same week as I did.

So we drive up north in our crossed ambulances, and one of our guys, Crazy Timmy, drives his own, old family trickster and we are all off. The first day was the drive, and then we settled in all the machines, weapons, and medical stuff and settled into our wide-open barracks taking a bed. There were trunks at the foot of each bed where we all put our personal things and put some music on the radio. After the cooks built up our suppers we got together in the food line and ate. After that, we all got together to receive who would be going where as the medics would split around to cover all units and tomorrow would be an early wake-up.

I was assigned to a group from Kankakee, and they had an older sergeant who spent time in the Vietnam war in the infantry. It was easy to work with him and his group. They all were serious about their work. So we ran a mile the next morning, had breakfast, and we all went to our own unit as a medic. We worked on using a compass to find specific spots and mark them off on a chart successfully. Then we moved on to the next mapped spot. There were some tough spots like going through swamp areas and confusion when we couldn't stay with the compass. Getting around our blocked area and getting back on course would find our destination. Yay! I had just a few minor injuries with these tough soldiers and it was easy to hang out for the beginning of our twelve-hour work.

One of the nights we had to stay awake for a possible *enemy* attack. I didn't go in a tent, a few were watching out, but I hid in our back end under a truck with my M-16 ready to fire. At around 2:00 a.m., I heard some slight-sounding movement from where I was hiding. Soon there were four to five enemies coming from the back, and I shot them dead…with blank bullets and saved our troop. The medic saved the troop! It was very cool for my first work outside of boot camp and Fort Sam Houston. I got along with the guys and they appreciated when I worked my butt off when I didn't have to and that was because I wanted to be worthy. The staff sergeant gave me nothing but solid appreciation. He even put me up for the "Soldier Who Works the Hardest" at the end of our time at Fort McCoy, but I didn't get it. The sergeant highly requested to have me, and I was glad to be with them all again the next year.

Cubans

From April 15 to October 31, 1980, hordes of refugees crossed the US border by sea called The Freedom Flotilla. Approximately fifteen thousand Cuban refugees flooded Fort McCoy, an active duty army installation, as a part of the greater resettlement effort. This marked the beginning of an event that would change the perception of the United States military for the rest of time. This was a memory to move our Joliet troops to help in any way we could. The vast amount of people was to be fenced in with barbed wire in some sections. On May 29, 1980, the first wave of refugees arrived. Preparation had been underway for nearly a month, with hospitals, quarantine areas, detention centers, and dining facilities had all been established.

Every refugee was seeking a sponsor in the US to get a job and a place anywhere in the country to live. However, the overcrowding of refugees made some to be frustrated and felt like being in a prison. A negative experience in the single male compound was ripping down seven thousand feet of eight-foot high fence. This was when riots began in some compounds. Fort McCoy had constant guards all around at all hours, ready, armed, and totally engaged. It was an important time in the process. Before we all left, there had been two Cubans who had run away, but being unable to speak English and the lack of any transportation, they didn't get very far.

Through a partnership between civilians and the military, the Cuban resettlement was possible, albeit at a large expense to the local communities, and military readiness at crucial training facilities such as Fort McCoy. What we did as medics was to help out families and their children who were in need of necessary medicines, shots, and basic health and check-ups for heart and any injuries.

Tank story

We had a chunky medic who drank too much in the evening if we weren't out in the field late. Especially me the first couple of years. Chunky would be really loud when many were trying to sleep in our open bed quarters. He just kept on making unworthy yelling and somewhat singing before he could fall asleep, so one similar Chunky night four of us tied his hands and feet onto his bed and hauled the big guy outside putting him straight in the path of the tanks that would be coming out at dawn. We heard them from inside loudly going klickity klack, klickity klack. The coming tanks heard Chunky yelling, "Stop! I've fallen, and I can't get out!" We all heard anxiously the same sound. Walking out the door, we see Chunky with some tankers outside just looking at him for a while and laughing like crazy. The rest of us went and joyously soaked up the poor guy's experience and untied him. He was in a bit of shock for a little time, and he never ever was loud at night in the quarters…at least for a couple of years.

Fort Campbell

To further hone its combat capabilities, the Joliet Illinois Army National Guard was driven down and flew down there where they were known as the "Iron Brigade." We worked alongside the 101st Airborne Division (Air Assault) for its first time Warfighter exercise of the year. I flew down with two other of our medics. Our pilot was a Vietnam war vet chopper pilot who was a bit wacky and cool at the same time. He flew along with our convoy for any possible negative breakdowns. As we were halfway down the way to Campbell, he landed in a field between wires, across from a McDonalds. He wanted coffee, two Big Macs, and anything we wanted. Quite the cool ride down. It wasn't legal to drop us where we dropped!

Chiggers are tiny mites that live outdoors in grassy or wooded areas near water. They thrive in warm temperatures, especially during the summer months, and attach to your clothes and bite your skin. Chigger bites cause itching at the site of the bite, commonly near the seams of tight-fitting clothing. They were a big problem. They could bite you anywhere and I seemed to be bit in the butt every time I sat down. Sometimes it wouldn't be felt right away. They would be in overgrown fields of grass, wooded areas, and moist soil near water. This was all anywhere we infantry soldiers would be the whole time there. Oh, and you had to stay away from things like black widow spiders, brown recluses, and what was called a wolf spider. Delightful warnings. Just think that in real warfare. There is more than just fighting the enemy soldiers, but multiple other things in the field also.

It was a humid, hot July when we settled with "Death from Above," which was the symbol sign for the 101st Airborne. From starting the loading of weapons/ammo and equipment from hundreds of miles away we were showing success or not in the movement. We were solid. Starting our time there we were being evaluated by troops from Fort Campbell who evaluated all of us in our skills, readiness, morale, and hard work in field exercises as well for sure of weapon's ability from pistols to heavy artillery as a unit. The firing was where we medics worked with pistols, rifles, and some machine guns but we were mostly there to be of medical support.

Frozen at Fort Mccoy

We once had a "ten day" at Fort McCoy in the middle of January. This was in tents, or should I say intense? We paraded up to the Fort and the first day was twenty-eight below zero. We all had to set up tents before the cooks would make supper. The medics had a fairly large tent that held five or six of us, and as we finally put it up, we brought in our cots, which had folded wood to hold up the cots, and that is where we slept.

We and all the troops had Smurf-like boots to wear in the terrible cold. We could air up the boots to help keep out the cold. To tell you the truth, even outside for a bit of minutes, my feet would be sweaty and warm. Inside the tent, we had two stoves from outside shooting heat inside. By the second or third day, we had a very dry floor that actually had tiny friends…called mice. It was a big deal though as it stayed in the lower forties inside. Starting on the fourth day, the wind picked up, and the temperature always stayed right around thirty-five below until about the seventh day when the low temp was *only* down to thirteen below.

There was very little action because the trucks were frozen up and maintenance troops were working on the trucks. There was no action in playing *war* or any firing range. The cooks were brought to one of the barracks and they made it a kitchen to bring food to the tents. We as medics were pretty busy as there were many people with frostbite. Frostbite causes a loss of feeling and color in the affected areas. It most often affects the nose, ears, cheeks, chin, fingers, or toes. Frostbite can permanently damage body tissues, and severe cases can lead to amputation. We had no amputations, but the definition above is what we were going through.

After everyone loaded up what they came with, the medics and cooks and weapon protectors and frostbitten got what they needed and the jeeps and trucks were running…all were ready to come home.

Fort Benning

The Airborne and Ranger Training Brigade conducts transformational training to develop and deliver competent and capable Rangers, Parachutists, Jumpmasters, and Reconnaissance Leaders to enable the US Army and the Joint Force to prevail in combat.

We worked under the Rangers at Fort Benning. Tough guys tried to make us tough. It was pretty much training and being evaluated for weaponry, leadership, and ability to follow directions clearly. There were some interesting war effects with false bullets, of course. We also got to examine the Rangers in duty as well as jumpers in jumping practice.

We spent a few days in the woods as medics and were warned about the snakes and copperheads like at Campbell, but this time, we came across a group of young copperheads who are more dangerous than the adults. Catching it quickly where we tented was good, but I put pictures in my mind at sleep time. They also have Caneback Rattlers that we avoided. Other things to look out for in hot and humid Georgia would be rabies from coons, foxes, coyotes, and bobcats. All those are in Minnesota. Of course, the worst would be big mosquitos, ticks, and a bug that bites very hard and was hard to even see, only the red spots on your butt or wherever.

We medics did have the opportunity to take the weekend and go down to Panama City. Of course, with the wild guys, they did anything you could think of and more. I actually chilled out by hanging on the beach, eating a couple of good meals, and hanging out on the deck in the evening. Then we rushed back to Benning and got everything packed and ready to follow the troops on the long drive back to Joliet.

What really ticked me off was the fact that I was told my grandfather Sam had passed away, and the funeral was four days ago. Not giving me the chance to be there with my dad and family was crap. I would see my grandpa all the time because he lived so close. It was a very negative memory that had a part in me walking away from the National Guard when I was an E-7, which was almost as high as I could go. It also led to me dropping out in my second sign-up, the eighth year of service, because I didn't meet the requirement of losing twenty-five pounds to get my retention bonus. So I turned in all my gear and *paid* for a couple of things I kept.

Rialto Theatre

Coming *home* when I had nowhere but to stay with my dad in an apartment out by Dellwood Park. Just downstairs from us were three slightly older guys with one as a Vietnam army warrior who got into heavy drugs while in war. He was totally deep into cocaine, heroin, and almost everything else and selling it every once in a while. JB was pretty much the biggest cocaine seller in Will County, and he was an old friend of mine, and I still pray for him.

JB had taken over the house he grew up in, and the parents were very close by and probably gave him the house because of his wife and child JB JR. He had a gun in every room of the house, so he said because he was paranoid that any people trying to steal drugs or the police would come in and arrest him. These were my worst days and I am sure the same for JB. I didn't work for a while and just took in my monthly National Guard money, so I became a part of the negative work for a short time.

Eventually, I started working for the famous and beautiful Rialto Theatre which is old but famous for all kinds of attractions. One of the top managers whose family ran the place and used drugs himself would often bring a couple of ferrets that he would let run around the theatre when nothing else was going on. The little stinkers would sneak up into the bottom of your pants if your pants weren't tight. This is the place where I was able to take an old, gold-painted music stand that was used in the 1920s, and I still have it today!

This was the place where a few of us were expected to take care of cleaning and buffing the marble columns and floors before a show. The giant crystal chandelier was a long time to clean as it needed to be brought down to cleanse and dry off before putting it back up.

Buffing and waxing was not such a trouble to keep the floors super sharp. Yet that chandelier was supposedly the biggest chandelier *not* in a museum but in the country. We also took care of the green room downstairs for musicians and actors preparing in the mirrors. There were also special rooms for the high-class people who needed specific foods and their own rooms. There was one room up for each person to the third level if needed.

One day we had a janitor, Jose, who came huffing and sweating and fearful about what just happened. He had cleaned all the mirrors downstairs and before he started to come back up there were multiple mirrors filled of small hand marks. Poor Jose freaked out! On the way up the stairs, a bright light came on, and when we went back to check the light, we found there was no battery connected to it, and it was impossible for it to light up. I didn't tell Jose that one. A few of us would often hear doors slam going up the single rooms three levels up aside from the main stage. There was no one up there and only one way to get there.

I also was able to get the posters of coming stars on the stage and the office staff would help me to have some autographs on singers and actors with most of them being stars from years past. These were the years I was always going with other workers to hit the bars in the late nights. Charlie's Irish Bar was real close by and just across from the Will County Jail. Go to Charlie's and you would be secretly allowed to go in the basement, and you would get cocaine for a price. Joliet in those days had drugs being sold off the streets in multiple places in Joliet as well as in bars.

There was an old guy who was always at Charlie's, and I would talk with him quite a bit. We would get to talking about Jesus and the Bible, and he took to it all the time. I asked him if he would go to church with me, and he said okay, but the two times I went to pick him up there was no one at the door of his apartment. Another old guy from the theatre talked with me before I went up to Crown College, and he was sure I was gonna be a preacher!

These songs were written many years ago and in the middle of my struggle with drugs and alcohol.

Dark Waters

Am   **G**
No waves can wash away the dreams
  F   **Am**
That haunt me in my memory.
             G
For I have wandered from dark waters,
  F   **Am**
A shadow to my transformed being.

      Dm
      For I have lived with the enemy,
        Am
      And I have dined in his halls.
      Dm
      I have slept with his daughters,
        E
      And I have listened for his calls.

Am   **G**
The weariness has left a trail
F   **Am**
Imprinted on my cheeks and soul.

G
Silence answered my cries for help,
F   **Am**
As my oppressors echoed shouts of glee.

    Dm
    Hope had drowned, my will was gone.
    Am
    Overwhelming odds prevailed.
    Dm
    When a graceful light empowered me,
    E
    Now forgiven, where once failed.

Am   **G**
Now living water fills my heart.
F   **Am**
My soul restored and joy reborn.
Light shining in a darkened place.
F   **Am**
No works were needed, all by grace.

I Can See the Lord in My Life

     Am   **Dm**

V1   It came upon the day when I could finally say,

     G   **C**

    "I no longer live according to the world's ways."

     F   **Dm**

    A time when all my sin, to God, would be erased

     E   **Am**

    By the pain-stained wood below my loving Savior's face.

    Am   **Dm**

V2   By faith, a gift from God, we're reckoned righteous in His eyes,

    G   **C**

    All because a humble servant took our cross and died…

    F   **Dm**

    Foreknown, predestined, called, and just, we all shall be glorified.

    E   **Am**

    First fruits, the Holy Spirit, given proof to be our guide.

Refrain

    Dm

    I can see the Lord in my life.

    G   **C**

    I believe in the Lord in my life.

F   Dm
Though I long tried to hide from His sight,
E   Am
I can now see my Lord.

    Am   Dm
V3 He saved me from a life of everlasting gloom.
    G   C
    Such love, grace, and direction, I never knew.
    F   Dm
    I thank you, Lord and Savior, for letting me be in you.
    E   Am
    I hope I understand just what you want me to do.
Repeat V2 and refrain

Saint Mary Immaculate

My change begins

Saint Mary was the best thing in the world at the time I was accepted to be a maintenance worker. I am *sure* it was set up by the Father, Son, and Holy Spirit through three Canadian nuns! Patricia was the principal for a long time at the school. I did custodial work every day, fixing toilet parts, keeping track of the furnaces, painting at the nun's house, and cleaning out the gutters. My dad Howie even came to help me work on a hard job replacing a major water connection to the older furnace. Sister Patricia always had some other new things to do.

So after a couple of years, I wrote a song for Sister Patricia to play my guitar for her at Christmas. The whole staff was getting together for a little Happy Jesus party, and I played my song. It started like: "Doug, there's a note on your door...I know you have a lot to do but I got a lot more," and it would go on with the various new jobs that would be sung. This truly was almost every day. Well, the melody was loved by everyone and Sister Pat had nothing but smiles, and they all were laughing. I'll be so happy to see the sisters in heaven someday. They were more than great.

Sister Mary was a fourth-grade teacher close to my age. She took over as principal the last 2 years of my time there and Patricia was kind of *retired* but worked in Joliet helping older sisters. I remember Mary asking me if I wanted to break work in the school summer and come over to the house to watch the Cubs and have a beer! Yes, I did go over a couple of times, but I always "had a lot of work to do" as the song went.

Barb was once a nun but got away from it and worked on going through a master's in education and special needs children. Another teacher was Angela, and she was a third-grade teacher. Both of these ladies became cool connections as friends, and they had a strong faith in Jesus while working with children. We also got together often to go to some concerts and movies and different birthday parties. We were close friends and all three of us survived the 280 mph tornado in Plainfield, Illinois.

But my dear sweet Sister Mary did not, and it was so sad and hurtful as was Gloria who was the music teacher and only at the school for less than two years. Because I loved music, I got to know her a bit and played guitar with the kids in church at times or in class. Going to the funerals of those two was nothing but tears. I had already lost many friends when I was younger. Lastly, my apartment neighbor from school went flying down the long hallway during the tornado and was thrown in her own room and rolled up in a rug while ending in a wide closet. A major vein in her thigh was bleeding fast, and until she was found and saved by the ambulance bringing her in a fast drive to St. Joe Hospital, she survived. This was not long after my dad died, but God had a plan for me.

Guest editorial

Changed Priorities

By Doug Anderson

I was exhausted and angry. It seems every time there is any lightning, my power goes out. I went to work a little early that day, so I left St. Mary School a little early. It was a scorcher of a day, with humidity that left me dripping like a soaked sponge. I had to come back to move a piano at 6:30 p.m., so I looked forward to cooling off for a few hours with the air conditioning at home. My anger caused even more sweat, until I became distracted by the darkness and a loud pelting sound. Looking out my kitchen window, there were what seemed to be hundreds of golf balls bouncing in the grass. It was a hail storm.

I called my sister Lori to warn her of the coming storm and hear how little Katie's first day of kindergarten had been. I got the "woe is me without power" speech out of the way and said good-bye. Five minutes later Lori called back to make sure I was safe. She heard of tornados touching down in Plainfield where I lived. There was darkness, hail and some wind, but everything seemed secure.

At 4:30 p.m. my brother David called to check on me, as he too heard of the tornado. I told him the same story as I had told Lori and rehashed my problems of sweating and no electricity. I jokingly remarked that maybe the school wouldn't even be there when I went back to move the piano. Little did I know.

NO POWER for TV and too dark to read, I decided to do something constructive on this deeply darkened afternoon. I prayed. Sirens began whining in a continuous, eerie chorus. I worried that something worse than I feared was going on. I tried calling the school, but there was no dial tone. I hurried to drive the short mile to St. Mary's, but traffic wasn't allowed through. So I sat in my car and listened to the radio reports.

Plainfield High School was demolished. Reports blared that many homes were destroyed and fires were breaking out all over town. I went inside and tried calling again. This time I had a dial tone, but the school and convent were busy. I kept trying to get through, but the phone lines were messed up. I was separated from work, but what was worse, from friends, too. The staff has been like family, and I feared for their safety. I felt helpless. I wanted to be there with them if there was any trouble.

Failing again to get to town, I heard a report that the church and school were wiped out. I prayed it wasn't so. I thought this had to be another one of my crazy dreams. Persistent reports that Sister Mary Keenan, the principal, and Gloria Sanchez, the music teacher, had died made this nightmare a stark mad reality. Sister Mary was crushed by whirling walls of brick as she was severed from the grip of fellow teachers. For some reason I thought of Is 53:10, 11: "Yet it was the Lord's will to crush him and cause him to suffer...After the suffering of his soul, he will see the light of life and be satisfied."

Mary was someone I could confide in. We shared personal feelings and beliefs. I lost my dad to cancer earlier this year and often reflected upon my struggles to her, as she was struggling with the death of her best friend Mary Alice, who was dying of cancer. Mary Alice was buried just a week before the tornado. These last few months, Mary had spent her days and nights ministering to Mary Alice as well as carrying on duties at school. She was a true servant of God who had a generous portion of the fruit of the Spirit.

GETTING TO know her these last five years has been like reading a beautiful book. Yet turning the page, I find no more words. With my finite wisdom, it doesn't seem right to end it here. However, Mary is at peace and living in God's glory. We who are left behind suffer from her absence. But as believers we have "a faith and knowledge resting on the hope of eternal life" (Ti 1:2).

Early on the morning after the tornado, I went to St. Mary's to mourn and to help with the clean-up. Tears forced their way out as I walked by a ghost of the church and rectory and toward the school. Standing where the main doors once were, someone pulled a heart-shaped wooden plaque with Sister Mary's name on it out of the rubble. Reality started pounding at me.

The secretary's car was seemingly hurled through the school, as it sat torn apart where the hallway once stood. The surrounding field looked as if it had been napalmed. There was no foliage, and all the trees were ripped at the same level. House after house was demolished. Cars looked like they had been kicked and stepped on by giants, and they were strewn in every imaginable place and position.

Many people came to help sift through the debris and save what could be salvaged. Some came to me with tears in their eyes, thinking I too had been killed. Then it began sinking in that I was spared injury and probably my life. I had been working all day in the part of the school that was totally destroyed. Though it is hard to rejoice while in sorrow, I thank the Lord for his grace and protection.

THE ANNEX where Gloria worked had completely disappeared. Only the gravel on which the building sat remained. This is where I was to have moved the piano. Gloria studied theology and music in college. I attend Moody Bible Institute in Chicago and enjoy writing music. This common ground led to a friendship that had just started. I was looking forward to knowing her better and sharing more with her. "Do not boast about tomorrow for you do not know what a day may bring forth" (Prv 27:1).

Twenty-nine people were killed, and many homes were destroyed—with a $100 million price tag of damage. Yet with all this tragedy, there were countless stories of God's hand of protection. Jason was bounced around outside the church before finding shelter. Tar from the pavement tattooed to his back confirmed it. The high school volleyball and football teams huddled along the only safe hallway to be found. Marilynn's kids remembered to go to an inner doorway in the house as the rest of the house was blowing away in the up to 300-mile-an-hour winds.

Donna saw the apartments in Crest Hill disappearing before here eyes. What looked like a huge ball of lead came down and destroyed her car, but left her intact as her high-decibel prayer was heard. Ann was sucked down the length of St. Mary's hallway, cut by flying glass, wrapped in a carpet and dropped in a classroom. She, along with many, is recovering from injuries. There are many, many more stories.

Love abounded around the tragic scene. The Red Cross was wonderful. Neighbors and friends came to share in the grief as well as the restoring process.

Through all this, I can see that material things are finite. We need to rebuild homes, schools and a church. Let's not neglect to build upon the foundation of the gift of faith. For that is the eternal treasure to be stored in heaven (Mt 6:21). "Command those who are rich in this present world not to be arrogant not to put their hope in wealth, which is so uncertain, but to put their hope in God, who richly provides us with everything..." (I Tim 6:17).

Doug Anderson, a Plainfield resident, is a maintenance engineer at St. Mary Immaculate School in Plainfield and also attends Moody Bible Institute in Chicago. Since the tornado he has been doing a variety of tasks at the parish, assisting in the reorganization efforts.

All this terrible stuff allowed me to finish classes at Moody Bible Institute in Chicago and that turned me to Crown College in Minnesota and made me a teacher. God made me a wife, and we have three children and two grandchildren. Who knows what will be next?

So many parents during my seven-plus years were so tender and Christian that it just continued the "job" or the gift from Jesus. All the staff of teachers, many parents, priests, and sisters were close and great people. I went to St. Mary's Immaculate as a definite port of my growth spiritually and away from demonic traps.

Oh! A male student who ended up being an All Star NFL player and Super Bowl winner as a running back for the Tampa Bay team! MIKE ALSTOTT.

He was a tough player who bounced off tackles and plowed through tacklers. He was nearly automatic in short yardage situations due to his physical style of running. However, he was versatile enough to take any carry in any situation to the house. Alstott was voted to six Pro Bowl teams, making four All-Pro squads. A star from Saint Mary Immaculate. God Bless you all Saint Mary Immaculate!

Crown College

Karen and I met on the very first day at Crown. She needed to go to work in her tank of a car soon so I let her go to Professor Carlson who would speak about the beginning of being a teacher. Karen already had a bachelor's degree, and I was going to get mine for the next two years. She appreciated me letting her go in before me, and I saw her as someone very beautiful even though I was in my thirties connecting to any girlfriend was the last thing on my mind.

She went with me later before classes began, and a couple of others went to the brand-new Mall of America. It was pretty cool and checking it out was fun for us all. Coming back to Crown, I was in my small room with a small sink, and bathrooms were down the hall. My partner was named Britz, and I figured I was sent to him because I was older and he had a unique personality. At night time, he would brush his teeth and wash his face at the sink and make loud noises during this loud hacking and brushing. It would be a challenge.

Right away I got into walking and jogging every evening. I enjoyed the peace of jogging down to the lake and sitting down on the grass for a short time to watch the sun go down over Lake Waconia. Walking back to school was a time of praying. Other times I would gather with a small group of guys and girls to run to the highway and come back.

Also, I got into a group for playing basketball, and even Professor Carlson would play for fun. Playing my favorite sport came to a game where I came flying down on someone's foot, and it twisted hard and popped loudly, and it swelled up quickly. Sweet Karen took me to a clinic, and the hard pain kept me away from running and basketball for a while.

At the beginning of classes, I went to try to be in a choir. During my time in high school, I only had good grades in classes I liked but now the confidence and sticking to everything I worked on by the grace of Jesus was strong. So I went to the director, and he wanted me to look at songs I didn't know and sing the notes; it was not good. I pulled out my guitar and sang a song, but he said I should be good playing during the Wednesday Chapels.

You know what I did get into? I joined a musical group of people playing handbells. Who else was in this? Yes, it was Karen which just brought us closer and closer in a fast way. We were playing right next to each other struggling to *stay* in our lanes for fun. Working and learning to play my bells was pretty cool. Our leader actually knew my older brother Barry at Bethel.

We were practicing during the year too for a musical at Christmas and going out of state in the spring for multiple churches. Karen and I found a church we would play Christmas songs for, as Karen played the keyboard, but the girl who majored in music had a sore throat and couldn't sing, which left me to sing on my own. It ended okay, and we received a nice amount of cash which helped for sure.

Now going back to October my first year, Karen and I were totally in love! Yes, it was quick. I called my aunt Yvonne up north and asked her and Uncle Al if it was okay for us to come up for a couple of days. They were fine with it and probably proud to have us before any other family. This was spiritual land. We had our separate little bedrooms and spent time going to Lake Vermilion to be in awe of the beauty, and Karen loved the quiet enjoying the giant lake colors during dusk. After a couple of days were over, we went *home* leaving the one hundred acres of evergreens, birch, moss, and water springs all over.

Cousin Troy and wife Denise were going to be gone from their apartment. They were just married, and Karen and I both sang at their sweet connection in being wedded. Karen and I were able to have some peace and quiet while getting our wedding set. Yes, we already decided on marriage, it was nice to get away for much was going on, and we could start planning even though neither one of us knew how things would go financially.

Still not married but secretly accepting each other to stay together for better or worse, we went to Illinois during Christmas break when we had some time off from school. Staying at my sister Lori's family we had a good time. I was proud to show off my wife-to-be and brother David's family had us over and my mom and Richters and Margie all got the joy of our very quick decision! Karen also got to meet friends from Saint Olaf near Chicago while in Illinois.

I had an evening job, which was hard-working, packing, and taking boxes off trucks every evening for UPS thanks to Bob until we left for Rochester. Thank you, Bob, the workout was solid and the money helped a lot! There was a day I started to work when I took Karen for a high-class meal at Arby's. This is when I brought her a wedding ring to put on her finger as we planned for our wedding in the early summer. It was winter, and Karen lost the ring while I was having a talk with UPS. It couldn't be found. Did I get mad at her? *No!* I love her.

Later, after UPS was told about the situation, the ring was found in the parking lot, and it went back on her finger. One of the workers at Arby's had searched through all the garbage in the restaurant for it! God is good all the time! This woman was working, going to college, and making her own wedding dress and eventually planned for all the flowers and decorations. Her uncle happily agreed to set up food for the reception.

Karen and I had a beautiful wedding for a low cost. After the service, we had a reception with all the family and friends. Instead of a dance, we had a program where we sang, as well as having family members also performing.

It was a long day since we took pictures very early in the morning where we first kissed at Crown College, and we opened presents in the evening at Karen's parents' house with multiple family members in attendance. By the time we left for up north, it was already 8:30 p.m. Didn't quite make it all the way up there and stayed in a hotel. We then spent our honeymoon up at Stolhammer's cabin for a week. It was peaceful, and we were alone together in a beautiful area until it was time to move to Rochester, Minnesota, for the beginning of our life together after another year at Crown, that is, living in Karen's parents' basement.

Folwell

Looking at Folwell Elementary in Rochester, Minnesota, I was quickly reminded of my own grade school in Lockport, Illinois. My old school was like an old castle taken from the ruins of some gothic terrain in time. So was Folwell actually, as it had a limestone exterior with a baked red tile roof with those half-circle cylinders. The lawn was brief and only on the front of the building as the rest was surrounded by fenced-in asphalt for a playground and parking. My mind was racing at record speed in anticipation of my first year of teaching.

The halls were wide and high with a musty hint in the air. It seemed like every classroom had its own level, and mine was almost the highest. On the way passing first and second grade, there was a cafeteria, which was also a staff lunch room. The lunchroom was made of yellow cement block that was narrow and not very long. It also had no windows which was very conducive to a quick lunch for the kids to play. There also was a pop machine just for staff costing ten cents, and that was greatly appreciated by a graduate fellow who had a stipend.

My room itself had high cathedral-like ceilings which didn't allow the hanging of the kids' work (bummer). The wire did hang at a lower level from one wall that allowed multiple classes to put things up to show the special pieces in school. The surroundings had plenty of space and a curtain-like divider that could be used to put on plays. It also was used to split the class for team teaching. My kids did a great job with a couple of plays we put on, and parents liked it too. A cloakroom from an early 1900s fashion also gave unique flavoring to compliment the high-vaulted windows so that we could look out to the East wall and see Saint Mary's Hospital from our room.

Our first apartment was on the lower level, and we were close to Dairy Queen for a rare treat. This was very close to Natalie, Tony, and Hannah's little house when they first came up. We were also close to the Jolly Green Giant factory working constantly on their veggies. The smell wasn't too hot; it was *not* the best and became old quickly. This was the beginning of the first summer while I was having classes at Winona State University, and most days we were just adapting to our new life.

There was a time when our bathtub was puking up black slime, and it wasn't anything we did. When we called the owner, he came to take a look without letting us know. At the time he came, we had a washer but no dryer, and clothes were hanging up around the apartment. Well, the owner, Mr. Fenske, forced us to move out, and that is when our colorful little house came up near Saint Mary Hospital, and I think it was a little cheaper. Plus, we were closer to my school.

Karen and I had quite a positive time even though we had little money with my stipend of $1,300.00 a month, and Karen worked at a nursery school during the school year and a printing factory in the summer that didn't probably make much more. *But* we were in early marriage, and we found it to be sweet for us to get some food from Wendy's for a delightful and appreciated time together once a week. The house we lived in was our second house with two little bedrooms, a little kitchen, and a small, living room. Oh, a little bathroom too and a shower (kind of) in the basement. Lastly, we had a colorful long shag carpet in red, white, and blue. Can you picture the beauty?

The next summer I started making a garden for food in the backyard. It was the year that my brother-in-law, Barry McCoy, moved in and had his own tiny bedroom. He was there because they were trying to sell their house back in Illinois, but he needed to begin working at Mayo. He got to play some softball with a church to have some fun for a couple of evenings during the week. I even joined and played a couple of games as I remembered how to hit a hard single live drive but fell down at first base on my first at-bat, but I was safe!

So many of my classmates were just super kids and parents built up their children well. I had multiple doctors and nurses at Mayo for parents. One came in to me to *teach* about the male and female bodies! Katie Brown's mom was a senator in Minnesota. Another dad was a surgeon who worked on people with heart problems and was actually the top heart surgeon. I was able to go to a close city where I collected three cow hearts and the heart doctor from Mayo came in and explained it deeply as we split the class to be able to touch and cut specific parts. Cool!

I had hurt my arm in softball one day, and I had Lauren P. say that she could talk to her dad about checking on my hand since he was a surgeon on hands. Every single one of the students was by far the best class I ever had. However, all my classes in thirty-plus years were great. If you could look at my classes, you could tell!

I also used my master's project about working to build the strength and confidence in math for girls to be more intense in their study and be able to work in small groups to complete and participate and learn how to overcome problems. It was successful. I also remember the end of the year when they had their fifth grade graduation. There was the sweetest Down syndrome girl I ever met, and I knew her well. I have dealt with many Down syndrome children. She gave a speech that was intelligent and well-said without any anxiety, and all the people listened intensely to her explanations of her time at Folwell. She was so sensitive that I was not the only one to allow tears to drop. She was also a solid clarinet player in the band and was the spelling champion in the school. The only tough thing for me was I had to speak right after her. She couldn't be beaten!

Mrs. Schwinghammer was the principal, and she would have kept me on the team as she shared how my time working hard with the kids was super and the parents agreed. However, it wasn't meant for me. I found out later for losing my spot (that was promised by the county), but for some holy meaning, a new male principal took over and for a friendly, qualified teacher I was not accepted. Even though I was hurt by the situation for a while but not too long! It was meant by heaven.

Oh, and student Joe's mom shared that her son said I was his favorite teacher. Awe. This was after they had moved to Eden Prairie by the way, and I was having my second colonoscopy, and the nurse happened to be Joe's mom! She was the one to start the tube up my butthole and realized who I was, and she said she couldn't believe the way she would see me in such a place! Nor could I.

Anyway, Karen and I had to move out of our tiny house as it was sold, and we never got any veggies that were planted and had one more apartment that lasted until life changed in a cool way with a *very* good new school at Oak Point Intermediate in Eden Prairie, a top school in Minnesota. We lived in one of my brother in-law Randy's house or duplexes, and best of all, a baby named Annika was born! We were actually able to move to the upper part of Randy's next-door duplex to get away from the cigarette smoke for pregnant Karen. I had to make my coffee in a faraway room for my dear wife to not smell the coffee. It was one of the greatest days for our life!

Oak Point Intermediate
Great Gilly Hopkins

I had my first solid class read the book of the "Great Gilly Hopkins." It was a National Book Award, and I had read so many different award-winning books that I had of my own before I received my license that teaching reading was a perfect place for me.

Galadriel Hopkins, who is known as Gilly, is eleven years old and living in her third foster home in less than three years. At the beginning of the book, she is "Gruesome Gilly." She is defiant, smart, determined, and unmanageable. She likes to be in control of every situation and doesn't like to conform to others' expectations of her. Her favorite phrase is, "I'll show them!" She has learned not to get attached to people because they leave. Instead of befriending people, she thinks about how she can use them to get her way. Gilly tries her hardest to alienate her new foster family, but they treat her like family anyway. The more time she spends with them, the more she grudgingly likes them. She eventually realizes that it feels good to be needed and loved by others and to love in return. By the end of the book, Gilly has become "Good Galadriel."

As a child in the foster care system, Gilly Hopkins has learned to cope with the fear of being abandoned by developing a shield around herself that prevents her from being hurt. Gilly pretends that she does not need anyone, and she is totally independent.

After the class got into the reading and answering the questions about her struggles, a different type of test was to begin. Everyone would be able to fill in a spot to present the story with a play-like set. Some people could represent lawyers for either side as to who should be able to keep Gilly. Is it the sweet, strong helping woman, Maime Trotter who raised her for three years of compassion?

How about when Nonnie Nonnie came, unknown to Gilly, as a total surprise? She wanted to make a permanent and rich home for Gilly, her granddaughter. So it was time to find out who was the best. As I said, there would be two lawyers for each female.

Students would represent Gilly, Trotter, William Ernest, Gilly's mom Courtney, Care worker Miss Ellis, sixth-grade teacher Miss Harris, and a friend of Miss Trotter and a friend of Mr. Randolph. Also, there would be reporters to write what was going on in the court for the newspaper, and there would be artists drawing what was going on in the court. The principal and I would be the final discussion and all students would decide who Gilly should live with and why. It was so cool! I loved the way it worked! Arnette enjoyed it also. I won't tell you how it ends. Read it!

Reading for Children's Hospital

I created a simple form for parents and grandparents to sign at the end of the school week. Children needed to get at least an hour of reading of their choice every day. Each book would be listed and the number of pages would be listed daily. The more pages you would read the more money each student would give to the hospital. If anyone struggled to get the money, they would still get the points for helping the children.

We had a leader at the time from the hospital, and we kept in touch with her and listened to what our kids might be able to help create needed things at all ages. She had no problem with what we wanted to present to the hospital from the three school classes of the *Stars*. She also sent me videos that would give a strong view of what could be a sweet piece of how our kids would be able to help build the needs of the children stuck in the hospital.

All the kids were excited after hearing the above and some loved and were happy to read more and for a good cause. Students from Pat Pavelka, Melanie Fransen, and I were the first ones to try it out. I promised a weird thing to do as usual to have my sister-in-law Nancy who was going to use the stuff needed for my brown hair and make it blonde hair. For some reason, it ended up pink! OH well, it was for a great cause and people would stare at me sometimes. I kept the pink most of the summer and even had Karen braid it for me on vacation.

Nancy was also a speaker to the classes and gave them all a strong story of what it was like and how it was prayerfully needed to be able to get through. But Shayna was a strong fighter. She was also our flower girl. Soon after Karen and I got married, she passed away after a long, tough, fight with cancer. My dear nephew Matthew was the ring carrier and also struggled most of his life, but again, he was a fighter and both of those kids made it through with joy somehow. Thank you, Jesus. The three classes raised over $2,000 for the children's hospital. It was exactly $2,161.35 that was agreed to be spent on trying out artistic painting on the children's walls from money collected, and some were used for books for all ages.

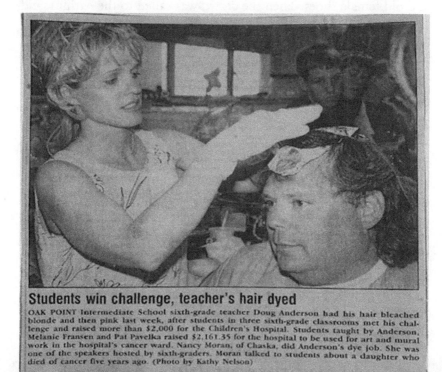

Students win challenge, teacher's hair dyed

OAK POINT Intermediate School sixth-grade teacher Doug Anderson had his hair bleached blonde and then pink last week, after students in three sixth-grade classrooms met his challenge and raised more than $2,000 for the Children's Hospital. Students taught by Anderson, Melanie Fransen and Pat Pavelka raised $2,161.35 for the hospital to be used for art and mural work in the hospital's cancer ward. Nancy Moran, of Chaska, did Anderson's dye job. She was one of the speakers hosted by sixth-graders. Moran talked to students about a daughter who died of cancer five years ago. (Photo by Kathy Nelson)

Children's hospital II

The following year there were many more classes partaking in the reading for children's hospital. The amount was much more to support straight to the hospital again. Talk about a lot of money. It would put together a neat room in the hallways that allowed kids at a younger age and elementary kids and also information for parents. Arts and crafts, music therapy, and items needed for infants, toddlers, and school age. This time I believe the total money used was around $8,000.

Now my present to the whole Atrium was to load up all the school classes that were a part of it. But before that happened, I had some girls in my homeroom to put makeup on my face and lots of it. Next came the wig on my head and an old lady's long skirt dress and old female shoes. Then the crowd was called to the Atrium, and I went out to have a dance with my buddy Todd, who was okay dancing with me, and the singing record of Mariah Carey. Don't try to picture this. It grew loud with laughing, which is just what I wanted to do. My weird look was enjoyed by the kids and teachers but mostly the kids at the hospital!

Bianca and twins

My wife and I had a unique connection with the three Roger girls. Unique and Monique were twins, but you wouldn't think they were. Monique was short and liked to talk a lot, and Unique fit her name well as she was much taller, and they had different faces too. They were the two older ones, and Bianca was a quiet girl and sweet. The first two girls went to Zion Baptist Church with our family just a couple of times, and they didn't want to go to a church that went at least two hours for singing and preaching, and praying would carry it longer.

The parent or eligible student may, at their own expense, be assisted or represented by one or more individuals of his or her own choice, including an attorney. I represented Bianca if needed and her grandma thought it okay. There were like four to five people in with grandma and mom was not able to be there for a while. So Bianca was allowed when we were going to Calvary Church in south Minneapolis.

We would pick her up most Sundays from Eden Prairie and bring her back home. Although we would keep her a few times for lunch with our kids too. The coolest thing was when she accepted Jesus and was baptized in a lake. We don't know where she is today, but I have tried.

Cambodia family

Pol Pot was the leader of the Khmer Rouge. Following the Khmer Rouge victory on April 17, 1975, he became Premier of Democratic Kampuchea and led the country in its war against Vietnam. Living in Cambodia during the Vietnam War was chaotic, rude, and murder hungry. Khmer Rouge soldiers were nearly hopeless toward anyone. The father of one of my students was once caught *stealing* a rotten potato to help feed his family. Because of that simple terrible thing? *Not!* It was demonic. The dad was taken and put against a wall to be shot. But his running mother came screaming and crying to save her son's life. He was saved. Thank you, Jesus!

The mother was pregnant at the time. Papa was walking three miles each morning and collected for his work in the rice fields, and their family could get just about what could keep them alive. It came to the point where dad wanted to get out of Cambodia and found there was room for them to leave in a loaded junk boat to eventually get to the United States as new migrants.

They wanted grandma to go with them, but she said she could not deal with such a long move, and they should go, but she will stay. Can you imagine the tears? Sad on both sides. The pregnant mom was about to have her baby by the time they arrived in the States, and eventually that baby was my student in Eden Prairie, Minnesota.

I got to know the family pretty well. The boy's father came to our class and shared this story, though he would be much deeper. We went fishing a few times near a big lake where a canal-like opening went to the lake. We would sit along throwing our bait out with a cast. The nicest people would have a picnic with my family and all the young kids. Karen and I were full of love for the family. I wish I would never have lost all the pictures of each class at Oak Point Intermediate School, it hurts. I can remember the many kids and picture their faces. It was my best school with much learning for myself and a connection to hundreds of children.

More from foreign countries

Yifan Chu was the brightest person academically and the greatest sixth-grade musician I will ever have mainly because she is great and I am retired. I know she played the piano beautifully, and I think her parents had her take string lessons too. After doing all of her Oak Point homework, she would go to work with her Chinese language. The Tiananmen Square protests, known in China as the June Fourth Incident, were student-led demonstrations held in Tiananmen Square, Beijing, in 1989. Yifan's parents were there and decided to make their way out of China and into the United States.

Yifan jumped from sixth grade to eighth with strong strength in all ways. Finally, while in high school she stayed short by getting through in three years to go to Duke University. I got in touch with her eventually to set up to meet her and have lunch with my wife and little ones as we were living in North Carolina at the time. She was up for it, and we were at least to talk for a while.

Yusuf came from Somalia, and I was happy to have him in my class. All the Somalians I had in my classes were great. Yusuf was a soft speaker, and he loved sports, which made a connection just right away. He had an older brother back in a Somali village where warfare was all over the place, but this is about a different kind of fighting. There was an old tiger causing problems often when one early evening Yusuf's brother shot arrows at the tiger, but it wasn't enough to break him down. I was told that the brother took the tiger by hands and twisted the tiger's head until he died and the brother became a champion in the village.

Yusuf himself was hit by shooting going on and was hit twice in his leg. The warfare was all over. He was never able to get the bullets out of his leg. In Eden Prairie, he loved playing basketball, and he was good even with the settled bullets in his one leg. It took until the end of eighth grade when he was able to go to a doctor and have the bullets taken out. His basketball got better and better with the leg stronger, and by his freshman year of high school, he had grown from

5'5" to 6'0" that year mainly because of the bullets taken out. I hope you are still playing ball Yusuf. God bless you.

Mohammad

I had Mohammad in the same class as Yusuf. He wanted to be called Moe instead so he could blend in with the people around him. He was a funny guy and a very easygoing person who had a smile on his face often. While the uncivil war was going on in Somalia and it seemed there was little control over the killing, Mohammad's large family left the village and went up into the mountains where they found a cave to survive. I don't know how long they all were there.

I also wondered how they got to the USA. I would guess that it was a church helping or some government setup. Can you imagine how *Moe* felt when he first got to Eden Prairie? Not only the city but going into a grocery store like a Super Target for the first time and just looking around to everything and everyone? All the food and clothes and TVs and so much more would be freaky after living in a cave. Can you wonder what it was like to enter Oak Point? So many children and sixty-four classrooms and computers and a huge library and sports and a beautiful gym and a World Cup swimming pool?

Withaniphone

Very bright girl who was serious about school but had a quiet ability to make people laugh also. She also worked outside of school at her mother's Thai restaurant in Richfield which was just four blocks from my family's house.

Withaniphone's mom had a very kind personality like her daughter and was extremely kind and generous. Karen and I *loved* her large stuffed egg rolls better. They were the best I'll ever get again and add the perfect sauce to dip those big diamonds of a meal. How I miss that food!

The mom was so nice to not only talk to the class about Thailand and how they got to the USA but she brought cut-up egg rolls for everyone in the class. She also said how much she appreciated her daughter working for her and to be a part of our school. The kids loved it so much they asked her to come again…and she did! I wish I could find many of the people I have known.

Carmen's story

Hi! As you can see, my name is Carmen; and I am from Quito, Ecuador. I had a fine mother and father, but we grew up in a poor country. Parents who only know the work of the market often see no value in attending school and are reluctant to let their children leave the market to discover a different life. The city was in a long valley in the Andes Mountains and a nearby volcano.

Quito served as the capital of the northern half of the Inca Empire. In 1533, the Inca general Ruminawi as well as another destroyed Quito so that it would not fall into the hands of the advancing conquistadors. Unfortunately, we were in a poverty area and had little chance to enjoy all the beauty, but I survived to grow up to a great life.

But one day when I was very young, it came out that my momma, who I loved very much, died and my father had a hard time working at the market and taking care of me. I was only three years old. So I was sent to my uncle's house along with his wife. He was not a nice man at all. Even though I was very young by the time—I was four years old—my uncle started abusing me in mean ways. So as a four-year-old, I ran away from what was called my home then and found a group of kids living on the streets in the 1980s and sleeping under bridges.

I was now homeless, sometimes on the streets, and abandoned with other children of various ages. I was four years old and had no family support. I followed other kids and would beg for food, and some would steal to get food. Some would wash cars or work for a cheap amount in the markets. Most people ignored us or gave us dirty looks or just ignored us. A high number of the children would eventually get caught by the police and be put in jail. Most other people did not think those of us living on our own in the streets were worth anything; we were garbage.

I didn't really understand what money was. As time went by, I was found in the streets by the police, and of course, they didn't know me. They brought me to an orphanage. It was called San Vicente de Paul. I went there and met people like the nuns, and one was very nice! I was put in a building with a lady named Ulalia. She was like a mom, but if you did bad things, she would hit you with a shoe or paddle or something else.

I also remember that if you threw food away, you would have to get it out of the garbage can and eat it. Guess what? I sneaked as much as I could and didn't think anyone would see me throw away my carrots in the garbage can. I was caught and had to pick it out of the smelly can and ate the carrots. Yuck! I still hate carrots unless they are raw. Not the best memory of mine!

I actually thought it was the best home I ever had. We had a large building where the girls who wanted to play could play with dolls. The older girls planted flowers in the garden we owned. We also could go to a beautiful field where we could play tag, run races, and kick balls. School would give us a snack at noon every day, and there was a gym for band and other things different from what Eden Prairie would be.

We got coins to buy snacks and lunch and got snacks when we got home too. We had school all year long. During Saturdays, we had church and Sundays also, but Sunday was a very long service time. We were able to visit other buildings also, so we could make friends there. If you are going to stay there all your life, you might as well have some friends! It is a comfort to have a good mom and friends.

When I was eight years old, I had a woman come and talk to me and told me I was going to be adopted. I was kind of sad and happy because when you get adopted, you feel special. But inside, I was kind of sad because I didn't want to lose my friends. But the lady came and signed the papers so she could adopt me. I got to spend time with her. Her name was Judy, and she became a wonderful mom; but before she was officially required, she had to go through a lot of paperwork. Judy had to fly to Ecuador, and when she came, we went to a bakery store and bought bread. We went through the market too and bought many foods I rarely ever had and some I never had.

So being officially adopted, my mom was more excited than I was and really sweet. When we were flying to America we stopped in and over a lot of states. We stopped to change planes too. One time we stopped in Florida. Then we were on our way to Minnesota.

At the airport in Minneapolis, my new aunt was there to meet me and my mom. I came with pants and a T-shirt. My aunt was there with a jacket for me so I wouldn't freeze because in Ecuador it is warm. I saw my new house, and I was so happy. I petted my two new cats named Trigger and Sally a lot because they liked me and were friendly. Where I come from, animals like these were very different. Also, after going "home," I found a friend who lived in the neighborhood, and we would play for hours. So my friend and I would sometimes find Barbie clothes. They were fancy little dresses. I still have some of them!

When I was twelve, I became a citizen of the United States of America after being in the country for four years. Eden Prairie is my home! I have a wonderful big family. I praise God for my life.

We brought money for snacks and lunch at school and snacks at home—kind of similar to the orphanage. During Saturdays, we had church and on Sundays also. But Sunday took a long time of music and preaching, not as similar as the orphanage. Boys took a bus to school, and I went to an all-girls school, so I was unable to know any boys.

I was the top leader of the band. If you were the leader, you carry the flag and hold it on your stomach right on your belly button. There would be three kids along with you who would hold the strings on their sides so the flag would stay protected.

I went to a school that wore uniforms. For gym, we wore black or white shorts and black or white T-shirts. It depended on what we were doing. We were unsure if we should wear shorts

or pants. It was a Catholic school and very different from where I came from.

I eventually went to Oak Point Intermediate
School. My teacher was Mr. Anderson, and he
was a super teacher. He was good at telling stories and the history of places all over the world.
Listening to him playing the guitar and singing
songs was something new for me, and I loved it.
He also brought out the class at break time to
play along with us. He set our class out multiple times with his wife, Karen. She brought her
four and five-year-old preschool children, and
our class would break into small groups to different stations and be *teachers* ourselves. Mr. Doug's
classes also came to teacher Karen's preschool.
Maybe I will someday be doing the same.

Most of the information came from Carmen's writing in sixth
grade which was back in the 1990s, I believe. My family had moved
around much since then, and we lost all the class picture copies of
my tenth year. It is hard to forget. I really hope I could see how well
Carmen is doing and how she has been. My prayers are with her and
her family as are very many other students. Karen and my family
have been back to Minnesota for quite a while now and shouldn't
leave.

Two years of multiple short one-act plays

Again, this is my greatest school to work with, and I even came
to Arnette about not leaving for North Carolina. Part of my wanting
to stay is how Karen's family, and mostly mom Angie, did not like us
all moving so far away from Minnesota to North Carolina. But it was
already set for Oak Point to have a new person to the great school,
but let's stick with the Eden Prairie School.

One of my hardest jobs, out of many, was two years of setting
up plays. Anyone in the 1400-plus kids could come into my room,

and we could talk about what they want to do in a play, and I would have a few written choices for them to memorize the short sentences before coming back. This would help in knowing what kids were serious with the lines. This meant that anyone could give it a try out of sixty-four classes. Was I *nuts?* Yes.

Well, I was shocked a little with the amount of students wanting a part. So I went through student after student for a week or two. Anyone who wanted to be a part of the play but not acting would be able to choose making or finding costumes, artistic people for background pieces, moving things during the changes, working lights, and bringing smaller items that would fit the play.

I wanted to bring in as many kids as I could who were serious about being a part. Therefore, I created two complete groups for the same plays that would be done on different days, except for the ones for parents in the evening where we would ask any parent to drop a dollar or two so we could collect shirts for the kids. I quickly got a couple of moms willing to help in practice so there would be bigger parts to be helped. Otherwise, small groups might be working on their own.

The first play was about a substitute, where students were not very polite as they tried to mess with the poor sub. This was a funny musical getting lots of laughs and a happy ending. Everyone worked so hard all the time. The players, those important for setting and moving everything out, and every other student involved were an important part. They had to be super proud of themselves.

The Second One Act plays were taken from five different African country folktales. They were delightful, serious a bit, musical, and meaningful. I of course set up two complete groups for each of the five Acts because I had a bigger amount of kids wanting to be a part. It again was a great night for all students involved and the artists setting up the backgrounds for the five acts couldn't be better. Praise God and all the help!

Monarch program

I was able to contact the University of Minnesota from 1995 to 1997 for the first time and get prepared along with the whole guided science process about observations, impressions, predictions, comparisons, questions, and feelings about the process. Starting meant setting a time in mid- to not-too-late August to collect about three hundred eggs with milkweed for our Atrium Star eight classes.

It would be easy for us to collect milkweed close to Oak Point to keep what we would need as the kids could collect them on walks in a specific way to keep them growing back again.

Before I collected the Monarch eggs, some pre-teaching was presenting information about the eggs and their shape and where it was on the milkweed. Just after we had the eggs, they would be hatching within the next four days, and everyone had at least two eggs to begin with a chance to get more in nature if needed during this specific time in August.

Next was understanding and explaining the nature of the caterpillars and the colors and sections to track them as they grew and understanding the molts of skin, and the new skin between the old is called *instars.*

PUPA: During the process of *metamorphosis* being on its way the caterpillars would spin their silk *chrysalis* for protection. I tried for the kids to write how it changed, and I would have videos on overnight to try and catch the whole thing in a quick process until we could catch one in process. It created a beautiful natural change within a bright green outer shell with sparking golden dots around it.

Soon it would be growing/changing within to work toward the final butterfly. The video part of the breaking out was such a wonderful thing to watch. It was fast movement when the butterfly was at its adult stage as it came with wet wings and needed to move them to dry out and be hanging from what once was bright green to a clear empty pupal.

Learning deeply about the anatomy, students would be done by videos and by creating their own drawings from egg to adult. Using small magnifying glasses for parts like the eyes, proboscis, body parts, and more was a blast. The butterflies were the kids' pet.

They would carefully learn how to light a tag on a specific part of a butterfly wing. All tagged butterflies would have their number recorded and I would send it in to the U of M. and they would send numbers that were caught in Mexico and let us know if any of ours made it as being caught. It was a long trip and an amazing one at that. These wonderful butterflies would be the ones coming back to where they came from the very next spring.

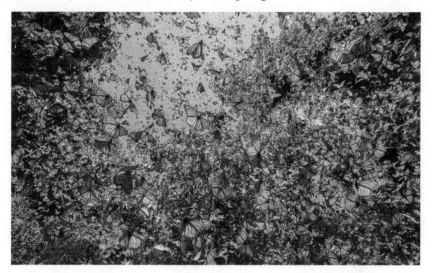

Lots of hard work

Everything I did was more than I expected I could do and the principal and team teachers did nothing but encourage my moving on with my ideas in education. I was crazy about being a part of the reading group that met to share solid books for our sixty-four classes. I *love* to read and was always bringing up stories that were deep and meaningful for the important parts of life, struggles in life, never giving up, people with physical and mental challenges, and comparing with them all. In my ten years at Oak Point, I brought in at least twenty to thirty new sets of books for the school and the classes to learn about reality and wonderful books. I loved being a part of this group and using the stories in my room.

North Carolina

Our house in Minnesota sold in two days. It was a comfort to us that we had made the correct decision. All ran smoothly in our preparation to move except for Karen's family. Most were not happy at all and could not understand how such a thing could be in God's will. As a matter of fact, I was ready to call it off but Karen said we should press on.

When we first arrived, it was through two days. Karen and I switched from being in the car with the kids to driving the large U-Haul with all our *junk* and rabbits. Going through the mountains as we got to the last ride to our destination, it was very dark and just pouring down and making it hard to see. It was crowded with big semis with many pulling aside, but praise God, we made it!

Our realtor had a totally empty small duplex that we could stay in until we found a house to buy. Dropping most things in a very crappy storage place that actually had water leaking and ruining photos, some marriage pics, and a few other things. Also, backing up with the truck to the so-called storage space, the U-Haul hit part of the junky thing with the roof of the truck. Storms, a hit, no house yet, school is coming soon? Oh well, all the time whether it was my decision or God's, we have to understand he is omnipotent, omnipresent, and omniscient, and he is in charge!

The next "wonderful thing" was setting up mattresses on the floor with the kids in the small temporary house and sleeping with each other. It was quiet. Poor Elijah had a hard time being a one-year-old in a strange, unknown place and in his young frustration would cry every night, saying, *home,* and wanting all of his toys. Nothing made sense to him. Things will get better. We also had no phone or real address, so in a way, we didn't exist in the eyes of society. Also, I was broadsided by a lady our first day in North Carolina and the insurance process, plus the repair to my car, while beginning a new job, was difficult in itself.

So it was challenging, to say the least, beginning in a far away, southern state with no one we knew. Add looking quickly for a new house before the school days start and that was soon! Franklinville was the little country school where I was introduced to Principal Vernice Willet and the fifth-grade teachers I would work with. Karen took a Kindergarten teaching job at Level Cross Elementary. We both started work the day after we arrived and the kids started a new daycare. It was a hard time of acclimation.

Being a veteran teacher, I thought it wouldn't be too hard getting used to a new school. I was wrong. All the little rules at this elementary were unknown to me, and I experienced them as I broke them. I also had four ADHD boys (one who was thirteen) in my fifth-grade class. The lack of respect and constant challenge/disregard for my authority really wore me down physically, emotionally, and spiritually. My esteem was very low as a teacher and only a glimmer of hope helped me make it through to Christmas. Meanwhile, as I struggled in all aspects of the first half of the year, Karen began a similar nightmare in the second half.

Being introduced to teachers in my hall, I got to know Big Girl who was friendly and kind and introduced me to her Big Mom who lived with her daughter and was close to school. Another older teacher had taught for a long time. She was great to work with and laid back and funny. Our principal was also old and she was a sincere fan of Elvis Presley. So to get on her side, I played my guitar and sang "Love Me Tender" for her and the other two and they all got a kick out of it.

Getting to know my school kids there was a good mix as there were a few who had dads in the military and they didn't get to see them often. Some kids were on the poor side of the tiny town and were close to school. Then there were a few who had a struggling home and were quite on their own and could have trouble often but I did my best to talk with them and pray for them. Otherwise, there were quite a few sweet kids who were always on task and easy to take care of what we would be working on.

Recess could be a treat and every once in a while there would be a fight but normally free time could also be weird. There were a few fifth graders who liked to play a game where they went out in the field and would spread out and then lay down on their backs. Why? Why you say? From their own spots, they would be trying to get the vultures to check them out from above and then circling, and then a couple would start to get closer and ready to drop to the ground. But before they would land, I would yell them away and the *students* would feel like they were successful.

The vultures are actually important animals as ugly as they look. I call them to be like garbage men picking up all the deadly food and eating it to clean the land. There was a garbage dump close by Franklinville and a larger one by Greensboro where the dump was close to the tobacco fields where an unbelievable amount of Vultures would be feeding. It was actually a pretty fearful experience that reminded me of a much stronger vulture army than Alfred Hitchcock's *The Birds*.

It was fun for the family to go checking out houses and the Realtor was a really nice Christian guy. Truman Snyder and his wife, Naomi, brought us to their church for some weeks before we later switched to the Covenant Christian Church. Truman had a great house for us and it was next door to his family through some woods. The realtor also had multiple animals that the kids loved and some loose animals that would come and welcome you and some fenced chickens and a cute Dalmatian dog.

When we went through the very, very, very super-duper house, I was totally excited and so were the rest! So much was happening. It was both exciting and a bit unsure.

A long winding driveway brought us to this house. Hidden behind the multiple types of trees all around us. It was relaxing and peaceful for sure. The kids all had their own bedroom as well as a bathroom in the same hall. Eli was getting his toys back and decorating them with a car/truck rug. Anna and Emma were able to fix their own rooms. Annika was putting everything in the proper place, and

Emma was just putting things in her messy best. Funny how when she was married, everything seemed to be well decorated, sweet, and clean with everything in a thoughtful specific place.

The hardest thing bringing into the 2,500 feet square one-level house was the piano we had to carefully drag it up eight steps and force it through the front door to bring it straight into the "music room." It was a room where we had a gas fire for such a beautiful sight and feeling, a couple of keyboards, recorders, my guitars, a record player, albums, CDs, a sofa to relax upon, my dad's clarinet and sax! Music Room. Listen, play, sing, or just chill.

There was a smallish den that was open-ended but helped enough to hold some bookcases, a desk, and a computer for work for school or contacting family. The window would allow you to watch kids playing out front or on the porch. A large wide-open space used as a dining room ended up getting a recent, strongly built picnic table for our meals (I wish we could have kept it). Our pantry had a door and inside there was plenty of space, at least four shelves on each wall, and there were still multiple cabinets in the kitchen. The floor in that whole area was multiple shapes of flint stone (no pun), which made it high-class.

All the doors were antique as were the door handles. The main inside walls were made of half-cut logs. The main bedroom was welcomed with a king-size and fancy wooden bed and my smaller beautiful dark wood dresser. It all fit the house perfectly. Never will I have such a house until heaven! But I miss it. I wish we could have brought that to Minnesota. In our connected bathroom, we had an old claw foot tub, as well as a separate shower. A long antique chest was remodeled with two sinks and a large mirror with drawers for any other needed pieces. I'll never forget being able to sit back in bed and watch out the bathroom window the show of the sun slowly disappearing at sunset. It was like being close to heaven.

There were beautiful rose bushes, and I was sure to plant some if we ever moved. Other flowers were in the back where there was a small wall that protected them. Still pretty flowers. We had a covered hot tub on a cement floor that we eventually got heated, and we all jumped in together. We could just sit there and listen to all the different birds and that Carolina sky was almost always a treat.

There were very friendly geckos! I loved the summer, and I would take a blanket and lay down on the driveway and watch the geckos as much as my book. I think Grandma Angie actually had a gecko on her bedroom wall while visiting.

When we first moved into our house, we were out back with a bonfire making s'mores. It was fairly dark outside and little one Eli was starting to mess with his little plastic chair. He slipped and fell toward the fire, and his hands were burnt to the point we had to get him to the hospital. His hands were treated with ointment, along with loose gauze for quite a while before they were back to being normal.

The one big guy who had failed school two times was about my size, and my size was big at that time. Being at least two years older than the class kids who spent a lot of time out, and about until late at night, he would often be out to steal. He had a poor home situation with just his mom, and money was weak. How many kids are like that? Sadly, there were too many.

He had too much frustration, and I could easily tell he did not have much hope for himself. Poor kid felt he would never be successful. North Carolina still allows corporal punishment as a form of discipline. So, no, it is not illegal to spank your child in the state. It is within the parents' rights to determine how to effectively administer punishment.

So the day came that I had to go to Principal Vernice and the mother of the boy had to be there to witness. It was explained why he needed to be spanked. He was told to lean forward against the desk and he was smacked like three times and it was pretty hard. He did not make a sound, a couple of tears dropped out and his look was stone-looking to mom and me. Not sure there was much positive help.

Another fifth grader had a temper sometimes but was ok others. A troubled, angry mom came into the office to share her fury. I spoke about "Your son was caught at recess and he wouldn't quit fighting another boy. So to protect them both I needed to separate them before someone really gets hurt. So I pulled your young guy off and he yelled at me for it."

He yelled out, "My mom will come out and put you in your place!"

Another negative piece after the fight talk (no mom now) was when the principal was yelling at the poor boy, and she was frustrated that he was not paying attention to her. She then loudly spoke to him saying, "What, are you deaf?"

Well, it just so happens that the kid was deaf in one ear, the one she was questioning but didn't know about it at all. She talked to me later not to mention the *deaf* part, especially to the mom. She wanted me to protect her from any problems. I met later with the mom, who was angry with me as a Northerner and not a Confederate; she later was a little better. No gun at my head or fire at my house. Actually, the rest of the year went pretty well, but the boy needed some help.

On our first February there, I was required to take the Praxis Test II. Even though I had eleven years of experience and a master's degree in education, North Carolina needed this post-college test score. However, I became ill with the flu. I missed two weeks of school and the test. My blood pressure was down to a low 76/56, and I normally struggled with high blood pressure. It was about five weeks before I started to feel normal again. Because I couldn't take the February Praxis, I was forced to take the test in May. Since the scoring could not be reported until June, I was forced to resign from my fifth-grade position. I was more than happy to stay where I was and glad to stay there, but I couldn't because of missing the date from the test.

Another thing that happened in North Carolina was that we took my mom to Myrtle Beach, South Carolina for a few days during Easter break. It was a joy to see a familiar face and share the beauty of the ocean. When we came back to our house, we walked into a flood! The hot water hose under the kitchen sink had popped off and water had been leaking for three days. All the floors in the kitchen, dining room, living room, and hallway were destroyed, as well as some of the subflooring. Though our insurance ended up covering our costs and we had gorgeous new floors installed, it took over three months to get the money and have all the various work completed.

Another thing that happened was the carbon monoxide detector going off. We were told it was getting to a dangerous point. No wonder it was hard staying awake! We ended up having to put in a whole new furnace and air-conditioner too.

So here we were, neither one of us with a job (since Karen's position wasn't renewed either because she hadn't taken the test yet). No income. You know what though? We had finally come to the point where we just started laughing off all the little *attacks*. It was time to walk in faith and not by sight. It was time to practice what we read/hear. In a society where the vast majority of people have all their physical/visible needs taken care of, is there any doubt as to why we Christians have difficulty walking in faith on a daily basis?

Karen and I got talking with a vet about a tough female bulldog found wandering on its own out in the country and wondered if we might be interested. Well, we did! Gracie became a part of our family, and she was a toddler in the house right away. She liked to push you aside with her butt just to get closer to you. Eli, being close to two years old, was too anxious to get in her face a couple of times, and Gracie didn't like that but settled down, and Eli did his best to stay out of her face.

One day I was cutting our grass in the backyard, and Gracie was just following me around when all of a sudden, a copperhead snake jumped up and went quickly away from the lawn cutter while Gracie jumped about four feet high and went the other way from the copperhead. Bright dog!

Raking leaves in the fall, I started burning them in big piles in a few places up front. It was starting to blow around quite an amount of smoke, but I was watching it safely the whole time. I kept my eye on it. All of a sudden, a *big black snake* came out of a nearby tree and was a six-feet-long booger. They are not dangerous to people but actually are nice to be around for rodents and other snakes. Although I think Mr. Black Snake was happy with all the guppies in our baby pool water on the side of the house!

One day coming home I caught sight of a side-winding rattle-snake crossing our driveway. It was a worry for me and Karen know-ing the kids would play on the drive or the woods to build a "safe place." It was something to be praying for protection.

However, one day the neighbor's Dalmatian came roaming around our yard, and Gracie was on the front porch. Gracie flew away after the dog, and it took her about five seconds to have the Dalmatian on its back, standing on top, with her mouth open and ready to bite the neck! Gracie looked at me like she was waiting to get the motion of killing when I threw one of the bicycles to make her jump away. Finally, she got up, and the poor guy just sped away as fast as possible never to come into our property again. Poor dog. This is where Karen and I confirmed that Gracie was trained to be a fighter, and the owner must have just thrown her away out in the country somewhere before we accepted her from the vet who took her in first.

My next position was at the Greensboro Middle School. It was a large school building bringing most of the students from the city out amongst the death fields of tobacco. There were two sections of entrance where police officers were stationed to be aware of any problems. I actually loved many of the students and some that had negative backgrounds that caused them to struggle in such a school. I was teaching American history and also North Carolina history. It took me some extra time to prepare a class for the "I don't know" North Carolina history! Teaching in class and having a computer room close to use for working on projects was a good opportunity to walk around to see how all are doing and help to work on their topic if needed.

A very likable kid, whom I called preacher because he was like his dad who was a preacher, and the cool boy was one of the *many* kids that were respectable. Something that was a huge negative was that there was always a teacher in our hall missing for a day. We all had at least thirty students in our classes but the school was evidently not a place that subs would go to. So without a sub, the kids would be scattered in the other classes, and I would usually get four to even six extra kids if two teachers were out! They had to do work and sometimes I had to pick it out. Otherwise, they would have paper assignments from the missing teacher to complete. Most would sit on the window sills, on the floor, or if lucky, an empty desk. Sad.

There was a very bright girl who was a cheerleader, and one day after class, she told me about a certain boy in class who would sneak little bags of weed and cocaine in tin foil and put them in a specific garbage can. "It was hidden well," she said, and people would buy it early and would get it when in class. I had to contact one of the cops in the building, and he said he would check it out. He knew who it was, and I didn't see the kid for the rest of the year.

One thing that showed top ability was the middle school basketball team. *Wow!* Their multiple tall guys could really dunk, and they were fast/quick and they could shoot. They were one of, if not *the* best team in North Carolina. It was a blast to watch them work on the court doing what they do best.

I was proud to make it through the year as it was a challenge. At the end of the year, the principal, who was very cool, talked to me about the next year. He knew I had some struggles but gave me the option of coming back or not. He talked about how hard it can be in school but left it to me. I am surprised that I said I would move on and the principal said thanks for hanging in the year and shook my hand and said, "I hope you find the right place." He knew the forty kids in a class were tough to deal with. So did I.

There were quite a few kids that didn't have much but poverty and the home situations were sad. One of my students lived with his dad, and his dad would disappear for days and even weeks sometimes. Hard-core drugs were the *job* his dad had and when gone. Miguel had to find food and run around in the nights and just didn't have a huge need for an English quiz or history test. There were much more important needs in his life. It is really hard to see so many kids being dragged into the arms of demonic oppression.

Our middle school was at the dead end of a road with the high school stationed at the beginning of the country road. It was November 1, 2006, when the high school didn't know there was a small fire starting. It started in a chemistry lab, and everything began to be changed. The next forty-one hours totally blew up the whole building. The middle school where I was couldn't get out past the burning because firefighters were blasting in all over. But we were able to get by after some hours.

Firemen smelled strong chemicals as soon as they got inside. Flames blew up sections as air systems pulled flames across the ceilings. It was burning extremely fast. Too fast to save the building. The amazing thing was that one thousand students and all the staff escaped before the worst fires came on.

A student was and still is thought to be the one who started it. Investigators have not stopped trying to put away the pyromaniac. After almost seventeen years, the person responsible still has not been caught.

Christmas time was off

All the kids were excited to go to Greensboro during Christmas time and see a movie in a theater. We were close to where the movie would be as I was checking things out coming down a slight hill. Driving, I did not see the stoplight until it was too late. I ran through it, and all my family was buckled up. Thank you, Jesus! We were plowed into right away, and it was a county police car. It was going so fast. We were clobbered one or two more times, rolled over twice, ended upside down, and finally stopped. So much happened in seconds.

The officer came up to us all and was nothing but kind. He said, "That's why it is called an accident," after I had apologized to him. My side window was missing, and I remember getting little pieces of glass in my arm. Everyone had tiny glass pieces. I got out of the van and wanted to make sure all were okay, but there was a terrible thought of someone being killed. I tried getting out upside down, and Eli's belt wouldn't come off, but some stranger came by to help, and he cut the belt so I could get Eli out. Both girls and mom were able to make it out, though, they don't remember how they got out.

We were in shock as we looked at the mess. One of the girls was cold, and I think the officer gave her a warm coat or maybe to sit in the car. Was I dreaming? I know I didn't want for all to be checked at the hospital, but that was a stupid choice. Then we were talking…what do we do? Karen called a neighbor friend who came and brought us home. I don't even want to go over the insurance or what car we would have or how insurance went up!

What Is Wrong with the Problems?

Problems? Coming home from school and town with my girls, I turned across from our driveway to look at a house and never should have done it! Driving back a block, I stopped to check for any cars, and I saw none at the top of the hill and none coming up from the right. So I began to pull across to our driveway, and a car came flying much faster than was okay. I didn't know if they would swerve around me (which they did *not* do). They pulled around to the right from where I had frozen. They then flew into a tree and there was a dangerous crash. Problems, problems came and didn't go away. I ended up getting the fault mostly after three teens came flying much faster than they should, and I had two young girls in my car while they were being careless.

I took my girls to the house, left the car there, and walked down to the crash to make sure people were okay. Police could ask me what happened, and 911 was called, and an ambulance was quick to help. There was a teen boy and girl in the car and, maybe one in the back. I thought the speed and tire tracks would explain the speed, but I guess not. The girl was injured for sure, but everyone eventually came out okay. I was told that it was my fault for not trying to cross the street completely. I think my nine lives are over.

> No testing has overtaken you that is not common to everyone. God is faithful, and he will not let you be tested beyond your strength, but with the testing he will also provide the way out so that you may be able to endure it. (1 Corinthians 10:13)

Chapel Hill Academy

W ell, it all started when we planned to leave North Carolina in time to get to Sylver's first wedding, carrying a big baby in her belly. So we made it back to Eden Prairie with our young ones, and Eli was going to be the ring bearer. The wedding went well, but I don't remember if Eli, who was two and almost three years old, was able to go through with it. We stayed at Karen's at the Rannow house with Ray and Angie for a couple of days, and Karen just happened to see there was an opening for a teacher at her old K-8 school, Chapel Hill Academy.

Karen started encouraging me to actually try it out and go in for an interview, knowing we would be going back to Asheboro, North Carolina. I had already accepted a position at a Christian school outside of Greensboro and was going to initially teach science classes to elementary students. I wasn't really crazy about changing to Minnesota again, but it was my wife, and it was the place of all her family, and she was missing Minnesota.

When I walked into Chapel Hill I met the headmistress and Mrs. Stude (you'll hear more of her later), I answered all the questions, and they said they would call me back when they decided with other staff.

On our way home, Karen answered the phone while I was driving. She was urging me to accept their offer of another interview with more teachers. I struggled and was not happy for a while, and we continued the second day of being home. I gave in eventually to accept the interview on the phone with a group of Chapel Hillites. I was still thinking…wouldn't be prudent…and took the phone with an expectation of not passing the interview.

But once I started getting questions, I began to answer with strong information and feeling confident about myself. Of course, they hired me, and we had to plan to be there in early August and pack all our stuff in a long truck carrier. All our furniture, but not our picnic table, clothes, and musical things including the piano on a very hot southern, summer, moist day. Some help was given by neighbors, though, one teenage girl was just throwing things in the truck carelessly. Our kids were little then but did help a bit with light things.

So back through the mountains, we would go and meet the truck when we got to Eden Prairie. We drove our two cars with three kids, one dog Gracie, and two bunnies. When we arrived at a hotel, we brought all the living things into our room and had to put the bunnies high on top of a closet cabinet about six or seven feet up, and we all watched Gracie jumping high up to see the bunnies, and if she could get a little higher, she might have supper. She was close but no cigar—thank goodness.

Well, we got to Eden Prairie and started loading into storage lockers with anyone who was capable, and there was a *lot* of stuff in holding *again*! We ended up staying with Jim and Ann, which was very nice of them to take five people and a country dog, Gracie, who was a loaner until we took her in from a vet. She was great with the kids, and we found out she was vicious if another dog was on our land. The rabbits found a home in the backyard bunny house.

Mom and I had a mattress on the floor in a room next to the living room, and Eli slept with us too. The laundry was next to us on one side, and Ann had lots of school materials like games, books, plants, and more. The living room was full of big boxes, mostly ours, and there was a small TV and a couch. Ann would come down to the laundry or get school stuff often and leave us with some instructions. We all came home at a different time after school which took a while to have special eating times for each family. Otherwise, Ann was okay to have all at once for dinner.

It was difficult for a fifty-one-year-old man and humbled to have my girls upstairs and the rest of us downstairs. I had super tension and frustration as I ended up being a seventh- and eighth-grade

English teacher. There was really no specific curriculum, so I had to begin building a plan a week ahead since we moved up soon before school began. I did get help from the two Dans and Mrs. Walker who had the job the year before. She was later fired. Dan Walker and Dan Tripps were very bright teachers and warned me about some negative things and people who could use their power. There were also a few parents that could have and use their power. Both Dans eventually moved on to another school nearby from frustration.

But this was a struggle even more in our *home* situation even though I brought in books on writing and adding famous writers for style and making choices of what you are and get the kids really interested about and using examples from professional writers and use it for your own style and vocab. There was a dippy, rude dad, Mr. Grosz whose wife ended up being the superintendent who fired me after ten years.

I had Annika setting things up for me after school when Grosz came in hardcore without me knowing anything about him. He started as a loudmouth, telling me how terrible I was as an eighth-grade teacher. He checked my background somehow, calling loudly, "You don't belong in English, and my daughter was hurt by the ideas you had for changing some parts of writing! She is a great writer, and your suggestions didn't make any sense!"

I felt and wanted to smack the man for being so ignorant, but my daughter, Annika, was in the room, and I bit my lip to keep from talking to Grosz right there, and I walked him out the door without a word. I had a good time with seventh graders but frustrations with just a couple of eighth graders. Most were just fine. One of my writers won the Twins' contest, which had students write about their fathers. It wasn't Daughter Grosz. Also, there were some eighth-grade parents who said it was a cool way of teaching different styles of professional writers.

Teaching for many years, there was one thing I thought was very wrong, and that was giving parents the opportunity to be anonymous. They could write the good, the bad, and any ugly thoughts without being known. Ms. T., the principal, would then look through the information on all the teachers, come to score them all, and have each teacher come in to discuss how they think they have done this year. Give *suggestions*. It seems rude that teachers don't know who and why things might be negative without talking to the teachers face-to-face. One negative takes ten good expressions to settle down the teacher. Am I whining too much?

In my history lessons (I moved to history my last nine years), I used a text to gain the first understanding of the topic and to discuss and gain an understanding of both, or multiple, sides to examine. I would have students keep notes and answer chapter questions for daily points once a week. If we were at war, I would like for students to try and examine both sides and note what they do or don't feel about situations. Did it make any sense? Why or why not? I also had each student write a test with instructions to have multiple choice, matching, sentence answers, and a few three to five-sentence answers. This gets the student deeper into the chapter hopefully, set up the questions and have the answers. It was a fun way to test for the kids.

We started looking at WWII against the Nazis and the Japanese mainly. The Nazis were to destroy Jewish people through genocide and others, ethnocide. Such awful Satan-led sickness will always hurt in my soul. Between 1941 and 1945, German forces took six million Russian prisoners of war. Jewish soldiers and suspected communists were usually shot right away. Large numbers of Russian prisoners ended up in special sections of German POW camps. Held by the Nazis to be racially and politically inferior, they were starved and brutalized. In total, three million Russian POWs died in German captivity.

The Holocaust was Nazi Germany's deliberate, organized, state-sponsored persecution and machinelike murder of approximately six million European Jews and at least five million Soviet prisoners of war, Romany, Jehovah's Witnesses, homosexuals, and other victims.

An estimated 70–85 million people died during WWII, including military and civilians, both those involved in the war directly and those who died from famine or disease.

WWII Military Soldiers Come to Class
Chuck Lindberg

I used people I know to come into my classroom and share their experiences. Chuck Lindberg lived just short of a block from our house in Richfield, Minnesota. When I found that out, I went down there with Karen. He and his wife were happy to bring us in and show us many things he had about the Iwo Jima battle. He shared much about the walk up the mountain and how they were fired at all the way up, and they found a long piece of steel and tied their small flag.

Richfield vet's flag-raising was first

wo Jima Marine is honored with founder of Legion

File Photo

Charles Lindberg helped raise the first flag atop Iwo Jima's Mount Suribachi. But a more famous photo was taken four hours later.

Charles W. Lindberg is the last survivor of the first group to raise a U.S. flag at Iwo Jima. He and his wife will be flown to a reunion there in March.

shouldn't have been dropped on Japan, a perspective for which the Smithsonian Institution recently was criticized. "It saved ourselves a million men. Iwo Jima was tough enough," he said.

On March 10, the Marine Corps is flying Lindberg and his wife, Violetta, to a reunion of war veterans on Iwo Jima. It will be the first time he has seen the small island since he left it on March 1, 1945, after being wounded by a sniper. He received the Silver Star.

Lindberg said he would like to make the long hike up the 550-foot Suribachi again.

"I'll see if I can do it," he said.

By Neal Gendler
Staff Writer

harles W. Lindberg of Richfield, introduced during Memorial Day ceremonies Monday at Fort Snelling National Cemetery as the last survivor of the first U.S. flag-raising atop Mount Suribachi on Iwo Jima, shows no surprise at being mistaken for one of the Marines in the famous photo.

That photo became one of the best-known of the war and was the basis for the 100-ton Marine Corps War Memorial statue in Arlington, Va.

Another photo, less dramatic, shows Lindberg and five other 5th Division Marines raising a smaller flag on a 10-foot piece of pipe after their patrol reached the top of the 550-foot mountain about 10:30 a.m., Feb. 23, 1945. Four hours later, that flag was replaced by a larger one, for which Associated Press photographer Joe Rosenthal was positioned at the right instant to win a Pulitzer Prize.

Lindberg wore a metal reproduction of his flag-raising's photo on his blazer, and after the ceremony pointed to himself as the helmet nearest the top.

"People are getting to know what happened," said Lindberg, a 75-year-old, semiretired electrician. "Historians are finding out. I've been interviewed by more people — even German television."

And Lindberg is not forgotten in his home town. Yesterday he was a guest of honor, seated out of the rain on a reviewing stand among politicians, military officers and leaders of veterans' organizations. Next to him was George Washington Bentley of Minneapolis, one of the six surviving founders of the American Legion.

Bentley, 94, was an Army private from Montgomery, Minn., in 1919 when he and more than 1,500 others founded what has become the United States' largest veterans' organization, with a membership of almost 2.6 million. He and Lindberg are honored annually at the ceremony.

Lindberg was 21 and from Grand Forks, N.D.,

Memorial Day continued on page 2B

Memorial Day/ 'The first thing we did was to raise the flag'

Continued from page 1B

when he joined the Marines Jan. 8, 1942, in Seattle, after losing his job tracking cars from Detroit when war halted production. He found combat near the start of the long haul up the Pacific, at Guadalcanal and Bougainville.

He was sent home, then back to the Pacific for the first landing on Iwo Jima. "I was in the first combat patrol to go up the mountain, and when we got up there, the first thing we did was to raise the flag," he said. "One of our men brought it from the ship."

The flag went up, Lindberg's patrol stood exposed to enemy fire and saluted, and troops below cheered and ships' whistles blew.

"It was like a big roar came up over the mountain," he said. "A big shiver went right through you, something you never forget." The flag also brought the first of 73 Japanese from a cave 150 yards away. One was shot throwing a grenade. Lindberg and another flame-thrower operator killed the rest. Later, a commander decided to put up a bigger flag.

"Same place," Lindberg said. "They just took ours down and put theirs up. I didn't know about it right away. I'd left the mountain. . . . I went back to load my tanks."

He discovered the change when he saw the famous photo weeks later, in a hospital recovering from a sniper's bullet that shattered a bone in his right forearm March 1, 1945.

The three survivors of the second flag-raising were flown home to tour the country selling war bonds. Lindberg, who won a Silver Star — the nation's third-highest decoration for valor — and his group got no such hero treatment. They weren't totally forgotten: Those living were invited to the dedication of the statue, where they were generally ignored.

Yesterday, Bentley and other veterans were praised for preserving democracy by U.S. Sen. Paul Wellstone, D-Minn., Rep. Jim Ramstad, R-Minn., and the official speaker, Army Maj. Gen. Raymond Bonnabeau Jr., deputy surgeon general for mobilization and reserve affairs.

They addressed about 1,100 people huddled in rain slickers, in cars or beneath umbrellas.

Wellstone called the ceremony symbolic of "living up to a contract and making sure that we don't cut millions of dollars from budgets of our hospitals, our center right here . . . that we always come through for people that have served our country."

Bonnabeau said more than 40 million Americans have served, and more than 1 million have died, in 12 major conflicts. The main reasons they went, he said, were feelings of responsibility and of commitment to their families, neighbors and country.

Ramstad said the memory of those who fought and died could be honored by preserving the dream of "an America in which an opportunity is related only to the desire to succeed."

140

It showed success but mostly hope for the marines below. Chuck was a firefighter and would fire into cave tunnels to force out the well-protected places within the mountain, but the fire forced the enemy out or would kill them by lack of oxygen or burning them. Chuck agreed to come and talk to my eighth-grade classes a couple of different times. He was the original marine who stuck the flag. The Washington, DC, Memorial of Iwo Jima was based on some of the other soldiers to have pictures taken and added a large flying flag to be used for a picture that flew all over our country. Based on an iconic image of the second flag-raising on the island of Iwo Jima during World War II, the US Marine Corps War Memorial is dedicated to "the Marine dead of all wars and their comrades of other services who fell fighting beside them." Chuck traveled all over after the war, explaining how the soldiers in the famous picture were there at the time, but that other soldiers, including Chuck, were actually the ones who originally raised the flag on Iwo Jima.

DOUG ANDERSON

Uncle Rube Stolhammer

My uncle Rube was also at that very battle at Iwo Jima, and he ended up with a Medal of Honor for taking out multiple Japanese firing well-placed machine gunners and being hit himself once in his head. He always had to be checked when flying after coming home because of the steel plate in his head. Info from him, his wife Doris, and my mom Ingie will follow, and I used their memories to help me in my history class.

142

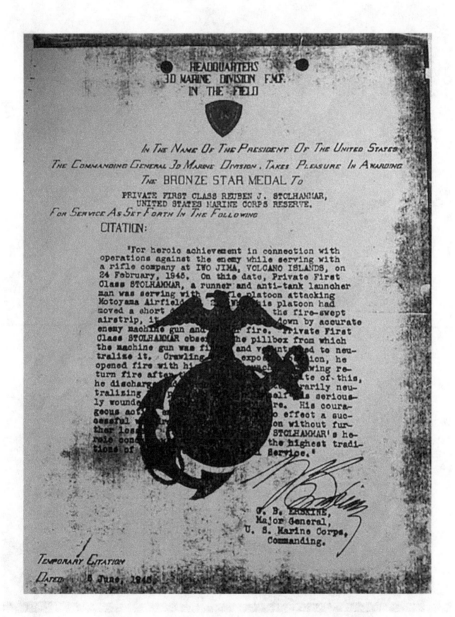

HEADQUARTERS
3D MARINE DIVISION F.M.F.
IN THE FIELD

In The Name Of The President Of The United States
The Commanding General 3d Marine Division, Takes Pleasure In Awarding
The BRONZE STAR MEDAL To

PRIVATE FIRST CLASS REUBEN J. STOLHAMMAR,
UNITED STATES MARINE CORPS RESERVE.
For Service As Set Forth In The Following

CITATION:

"For heroic achievement in connection with
operations against the enemy while serving with
a rifle company at IWO JIMA, VOLCANO ISLANDS, on
24 February, 1945. On this date, Private First
Class STOLHAMMAR, a runner and anti-tank launcher
man was serving with ____ rifle platoon attacking
Motoyama Airfield ____ W____ his platoon had
moved a short ____ ____ the fire-swept
airstrip, it ____ ____ down by accurate
enemy machine gun and ____ fire. Private First
Class STOLHAMMAR obse____ he pillbox from which
the machine gun was fi____ and vo____ted to neu-
tralize it. Crawling ____ expo____ ____tion, he
opened fire with hi____ ____unch ____wing return fire after ____ ____te of this,
he discharged ____ ____rarily neu-
tralizing ____ ____self ____ seriously wounded ____ ____re. His coura-
geous act____ ____o effect a successful ____ ____on without further loss ____ STOLHAMMAR's he-
role cond____ ____ the highest tradi-
tions of ____ ____ ____ Service."

G. B. ERSKINE,
Major General,
U. S. Marine Corps,
Commanding.

Temporary Citation
Dated   5 June, 1945

DOUG ANDERSON

with answers.

A. I was given an occupational deferment when the war started but as 1943 began to pass all of my friends were in active service and in those days if you were seen in civilian clothes and were of draft age people looked accusingly at you and wondered "what's wrong with you?" How different from today. So, about the first of November 1943 I decided to leave my job which automatically made me eligible for the draft and I went into active duty about the 15th f February.

B. The morning I left for active duty at that point I was assigned to the Navy and a Marine Sargent entered our Squadroon and said to about 300 of us assembled "I need 50 volunteers for the Marine Corps. Three hands were raised so the Sargent said "OK if you won't volunteer I will volunteer for you." We were standing in three ranks of about 100 and the Sgt. looked up and down each rank and everyone was trying to hide behind the guy in front of them. I was at the end of the middle rank doing the same and he said "you down there you are first." I looked behind me to see who he might be pointing at and the Sgt. said "no, you!" (meaning me) and I was the first "volunteered." In retrospect, however, I am happy for the experience.

C. The war effort at this point was at a critical point and there was not a whole lot of xxxxxxxxxxxx encouraging news that came through the Media. The casualties were quite heavy.

D. Boot Camp was an experience where the recruits, among other training, were being taught personal discipline and obedience to the commands of the Officers was absolutely necessary and profitable in the long run in order to survive combat. Again, how different from today.

E. We really were not aware of what was going to lie before us ahead of us. As usual, many rumors circulated about, but we did not know until we were able to make the invasion and even then the geographical location to many of us was not important. All we knew for sure was we were going into combat.

F. War is a terrible thing but sometimes it is necessary and the feelings of patriotism and fighting for ones country most of the time overcame ones anxiety and/or fear. WOW! How different again from much of the feeling of America today.

G. My first battle experience was on the Island of Guam which was a United States possession and had served as an intermediate landing field for Pan American Airlines as they flew across the ocean, so Guam was really a battle to regain and possess what really belonged to the USA.

The second battle experience was at Iwo Jima. Iwo Jima was targeted as an emergency landing area and strategy area for furthering the campaign to end the war against Japan. One of the significant reasons for invading was it would provide an intermediary landing area for long range bombing of Japan. Those planes flew from Guam and Saipan to Japan on bombing raids and Iwo Jima offered an intermediary emergency landing area in the event the plane was damaged during the raid.

222222

DORIS

A. During the war I lived in Chicago at home with my parents

B. I worked for the Treasury Department, War Bond Division. During those days many companies would hold War Bond Rallies for their employees to encourage them to buy War Bonds. They would request entertainment, returning Servicemen from the war zones and anything to encourage purchase of Bonds. My job was to interview the returning Servicemen , most of whom had been wounded and back in the states - many of them returning overseas. I would interview these men, listen to their stories and then assign them to companies sponsoring the Rallies. Our office also contacted the entertainers from Hollywood and elsewhere so we had a lot of well known people in and out of our office.

I resigned from this position when Rube realized he would not be coming home from Boot Camp in California and going right overseas, We were engaged at the time but my parents allowed me to go to California before he left; his Buddy's girlfriend was also going out there. I lived in a home with two "old maids" who were Seventh Day Adventists and did not allow smoking or drinking in the home and no gentlemen friends. That suited me fine and I had a very small room. When Rube went overseas I went back home to Chicago and looked for another job. Worked at the Rock Island Railroad which was interesting - railroads were very important during the war.

C. Rationing and stamps were part of our lives. We had stamps for food, shoes, gasoline and just about everything. We received a decal to put on the windshield of our cars that would show howmuch gas we were entitled to - I believe they were A, B, C. Nylon stocking were at a premium and if a department store did get in a shipment then was almost a stampede to buy one pair - and you better be there early. We could not buy any hershey bars - those were being sent to Servicemen. Once in a while a shipment would come in to the railroad depot and we would all dash down to buy a hershey bar. Butter was at a premium and I believe coffee was hard to get - those who had cars could not get new tires very easily. We did without and made do with what we could get. Peop did not complain - the war hit in just about every home and people worked together.

D. As far as I can remember wages were fair. Working for a railroad, our wages were considered quite good. I don't remember people complaining about wages then, they had a job and seemed to concentrate on the war. Prices on some items were high, but with rationing we couldn't get many food items anyway - meat was not always available. Housing was difficult to get, there was a shortage for many years after the war when Servicemen returned home, got married and wanted their own home. You were lucky to be able to find an apartment. I do not recall what the market for homes was - they were scarce for quite a while.

E. The mood of the nation was somber; reports from the battlefields were not always very encouraging. We relied on newspapers and radio for our information which took time to reach the people. I do know that people were joined together, worked together and helped one another. There wasn't the selfishness, ME, ME, I, I, attitude that is in our society today. We coped with whatever situation we were in because we didn't expect everything to go our way, as some do today. What we couldn't get, we did without and we didn't have to have "everything" like today - the war was uppermost in people's minds.

F. Many churches were open for people to go in and pray, meditate or just be there. The churches supported the war effort, sending gifts of food, writing letters, keeping in touch with their Servicemen and generally helped in any way they could. I can recall at South Shore we used to go down to the Servicemen's Center in downtown Chicago at least once a month and prepare dinners for the men going through Chicago. This was a Christian Center and there would be speakers, a lot of singing, playing table games and sometimes just listening.

2.

G. I probably wrote almost every day. We never knew whether the mail would be delivered in one week, one month or at all. I tried to keep him up on all the news at home, at church and also about his Buddies who were also serving in the Armed Forces. Sometimes the news was not good. There were times we did not know where he was but just kept writing and sending boxes of food, mostly cookies and sometimes canned fruit, to the only address we had. Our letters were censored, mine to him and his to me. Sometimes our letter would look like a dress pattern with all the holes in it where some word or sentence would be cut out..

H. Not knowing is always very frustrating. I knew what Division of the Marines he was in and could kinda keep track of where they were through newspapers and radio. By the time we received that news though he could have been long time gone from there. The one thing that sticks out in my mind the most though is the night I heard on the radio that the 3rd Marine Division had invaded Iwo Jima. We knew this was one of the toughest, bloodiest battles of the Pacific so this news was very frightening. I knew that Astrid & Bruce Fleming (Pastor at South Shore then) were going to be at your grandma & grandpa Swanson that night for coffee. It may have been a birthday celebration for Mabel because Rube's family was there too. I remember I called over there to talk to Bruce and tell him Rube's outfit had gone in on Iwo. Bruce was very concerned and, of course, told me he would tell the others and that they would be praying.

When we did not hear anything from Rube for a long time we just had to wait. They say no news is good news and we knew if anything had happened his Dad would have been notified. It was a very difficult time but there was a lot of prayer going on and finally one day I received a letter from him. I could see it was his own handwriting so knew he could write, he could see. This letter came from the Naval Hospital in Aiea Heights, Hawaii. The Navy gave him a chance to write home first and then after that came the telegram to his Dad saying that "your son has been wounded" - from then on we received more mail and he was then sent to the Naval Hospital in Oakland Calif., from there to Great Lakes Naval Hospital in Great Lakes, Illinois and was discharged from there with a medical discharge - 50% disability.

I. The first day Rube was given a "pass" from Great Lakes he came to my house. Of course, I thought he looked wonderful but I guess he was still recuperating. It was hard to believe he was actually there. I had a million questions to ask about all that happened since I had left California. We then planned our wedding. He was discharged September 25, 1945 and we were married November 24, 1945. The first thing he had to do was find a job, which he did but I was making more money than he was but that wasn't any problem. He went back to school at Northwestern University nights and things gradually got back to a normal lifestyle. When we got married we could not get any electrical items at all. With the money we received we ordered an iron, waffle iron, toaster and mixmaster. I ordered these at a nearby Hardware Store and as the item came in I would get a call to pick it up. It probably took a couple months to get everything. Companies that made these electrical items were all involved in producing parts, etc. for the war effort.

J. I suppose there was some prejudice - especially toward Japan after the bombing of Pearl Harbor. I really don't remember too much about prejudice, everyone just wanted to do what was necessary to have the war over and our boys come home.

To sum it all up, we lived in a different era. People worked together, helped one another. There wasn't the affluence there is today - we were all in this together and there was patriotism that we have forgotten today. The flag and patriotic songs were a way of life. People had banners in their front windows showing they had sons & daughters in the service or a gold star meaning their service person had been killed.

INGRID

1. Remember my mother trying to improve cooking & baking because meat, sugar, butter & other were rationed.

2. My Dad had [business] to [use] able to get a little higher ration of gas & tires. No new cars were built during the war years.

3. I remember each different fellow in my church youth group, by[life] service. Wrote to most of them on a regular basis. (Dating date with serviceman was every girl's dream.)

4. Much propaganda, though subtle at times, to stir up emotion & hatred against the "Japs." Much was done thru war movies, cartoons etc. Always depicting the "Jap" soldier with a diabolical grin. The Japanese people in general

were made to be monsters. The
Japanese American (citizens) were
taken from their homes & put into
guarded camps.

5) It really tore me up to see Newsreels
& news photos of our "boys" fighting
especially in the Pacific Islands.
Even now when I hear names like
Iwo Jima, Corregidor, Bataan etc.
I can still see the awful bloodshed
in my mind.

6. Had a real fear of being bombed
when I viewed pictures from England
especially. I don't remember there
being actual bomb shelters or bomb
drills in school

7. I was really afraid when it was
reported that German Subs were
sighted on the Atlantic Coast &
Japanese Subs off California.

8. I remember the horror @ seeing
photos from German Concentration
Camp & also hearing of the atrocities
against our "boys" in the Pacific
Islands by the "Japs." I was so
afraid for my friend from church

148

More Men Who Came to Share History

Another WWII army soldier found himself caught behind the Nazi line of fighting. He came to my classes two years in a row before his health was too bad. He shared his story before passing away and was a solid person. Seeing that there were a few Nazis coming his way and two were officers, he knew they were pushing further against the USA and European countries. Walking from a distance, he quickly laid down by dead soldiers and rubbed his face and clothes with blood from the dead. There was no other way he would survive. One Captain came by him and got the wallet from his pocket, a couple pictures of his wife were in the wallet too and even grabbed his rifle.

Late in the next day, things changed quickly, and the Nazis were quickly being pushed hard, and the Germans were on the run. The US was blasting them back. As weird as it sounds, he saw the same Captain and shot him down using a weapon he took from a dead person. He then saw friendly fighters coming too. By the way, he said he grabbed the Nazi's pocket and got his wallet back as well as the pictures of his wife. What a story to survive.

Old soldier George

Another army soldier of WWII was caught as a prisoner and was brought to a prisoner of war camp where life was miserable with nothing that was good. He came all the way there tied to the front of a Panzer IV German tank. By the time he was at the camp, he was worn out. He got very little food at all and limited water, and he lost very much weight down to ninety-four pounds after being 198, and it was all in less than a year. Again the US and some Canadians came storming into camp, and the Germans had to put their hands up, throwing away their weapons, raising a white flag or in any other suitable fashion. Isolated members of armed forces or members of a formation clearly expressed to the enemy during battle their intention to cease fighting and the Nazis would be taken as prisoners. However, many Germans were killed by not wanting to give up.

George was taken to an Army hospital to strengthen him a bit before sending him on his way home upon a Red Cross ship. Even then the medical ship was being shot at by Germans. George's nurse was trying to escape through a port door window, but George pulled the heavy nurse back and said to just stay down there. It is a crime to be shooting at a Red Cross ship. There are rules also known as International Humanitarian Laws. To name a few, torture is prohibited, prisoners must be provided food and water, and medical workers and hospitals must be protected. The ship, of course, got through, otherwise, he wouldn't be saved from attacks at our school to share his experience. He made it home and brought with him his crazy stories from the war, but nothing was funny in war.

Mary, Mary Quite Contrary

I must say that I believe that Mary Stude was the only one who didn't vote for me to be the new seventh- and eighth-grade English teacher. Elementary would have been much better. Many people had no idea of what my family had to go through with our things in storage, multiple big boxes in the too-crowded house with the five Andersons who survived.

I remember going on a walk from school with our classes to bag and box food for a country in Africa. For some reason, I said I worked at one time for UPS and did hardcore putting boxes on and taking them down at a very fast pace. So with that, Mary had to open her loud voice and yell out that "Doug would work with taking the heavy boxes with the boys." Didn't ask me. Just *told* me. I had no say in it I guess and the multiple fathers, twenty years younger than me were able to have fun.

Now I don't think she was awful but the first year she didn't deal with me in a very positive, helpful way at all. God stay with me! There was an instant that was a couple of years later when she said I could be in charge of the lockers at the beginning of school. *Whoopy!* Well, Hana V.'s dad had just passed away that summer, and it was a crushing, unexpected, painful loss for the large family to deal with. My daughter, Emilie, wanted to put her best friends next to Van, one on each side, to help her deal with the loss. Evidently, there were a few girls who were on Stude's volleyball team complaining about the changing. Mrs. Stude made them be in alphabet order always but never told me that. Of course, Mary talked to me with Principal Kathy Tweeten about how it was improper for me to do and listen to my daughter for the idea of helping a girl who just lost her daddy.

It was a ridiculous change, and my next move was going to the East Coast with the kids.

I was excited to go, and, of course, Stude was in charge with her sidekick April B, but I had Debbie to go also and be my protection. Believe me. It was a lot of places for the first time in Gettysburg, Philadelphia history, Washington, DC, that was loaded with historical sites and the kids waited to go into New York City where they looked so forward to the city itself and things to buy, a special dinner, and a Broadway Play!

One thing that was a struggle for me is that our guide was always late to go places we were supposed to be! We had to actually run/ trot for the whole group to make the historical Arlington National Cemetery. It was raining and the walk, I mean run/trot, up the hill to make it in time for the unknown soldier when the guards switch and our dressed up wet two kids are there in time to present flowers to give to a soldier.

We also were running through all the other parts from the Lincoln to ML King Memorial and Roosevelt Memorial and Vietnam Memorial and Korean. Everyone was wet and worn out for more than one day. After this first trip, I felt like I had been gone for three weeks and was so happy to see my wife and kids when we got back. Hugs and more hugs. I also decided I would bring bottles of those little drinks that were supposed to keep you with (five hour extra energy), but I never needed it again, nor did I have to run, nor have that same guide.

Trip Number Three Makeup

Later, in the third trip, I think that I was told to go to some girl's hotel room. When I knocked on the door and a girl opened it, they were *all* in there. Not only that, but also they all had like arm cut sweatshirts and short shorts. Boyer was at the door when I walked in, and I was stunned! The girls were all excited and because they wanted to wear the clothes to the Capitol Building with a guided walk all over the beautiful place. I can just imagine the look I must have had before I asked them all, "What are you all doing?"

"We want to wear these tomorrow morning; we've been working on these! Don't you think we could wear these, Mr. D?"

"Seriously girls?"

So as I look around I see that a couple have cut their sweatshirts so their belly showed. A few just had a sports bra on, so they asked me again, "Really, don't you think we could wear these?"

"Ahhh, I don't think so, girls. It doesn't seem proper in such a place as the Capitol Building and where many people are touring the place. But if Mrs. Stude thinks it is okay that is on her shoulder, not mine." At that moment, Stude comes out from behind the curtains and is laughing as she couldn't hold it anymore. The girls got a huge kick out of it, and the late night was over.

Rocky Balboa Steps

The famous Rocky Balboa steps in Philadelphia was an early place to visit the first two years of the East Coast area. Everyone would do the run up the steps and take a pic of Rocky's Statue, and some would do more running up and down after such a long drive. Some would just sit down and watch the city and talk and chill a bit outside. We chaperones would be scattered around to keep all the kids in vision. I was up top with a view over all of them.

Then I heard a girl scream down below, and one of the girls was injured and holding her leg tight, and other kids started coming to help her out. Stude said she would call 911 for an ambulance, and after just a few minutes, the sirens were screaming...two of them! They were easy to see now as they were coming right toward us on the steps. Since I had some military medical experience, I was down fast and saw both the ambulances just drive on by. I was trying to wave one down, but it was too late. Coming back to the injured girl I saw others laughing and I saw the *injured* girl also. Of course, it was another Stude trick at the first stop. At least she didn't mean it for me but didn't warn me either.

Mrs. Stude Again?

We were riding toward Washington, DC, and I was pretending that I was falling asleep, and I was a couple seats behind the driver of the bus. There was a group of girls in the back trying to speak quietly but not doing very well. They were talking of a trick on Mr. D. when he is in sure sleep. Planning to sneak up one at a time each girl would bring their own shaving cream and hair pins, some lip stick and other face powder. Waiting for a later time when the bus was quiet, they were ready to begin.

Anyway, it came time when they were strong/brave enough to begin their *trick*. Figuring out who was going to be the first to softly attack was finally agreeing to go and be number 1. She heard me snoring a bit with my head hanging down. So she quietly came close to me and messed stuff all over my beard. Number 2 was tiptoeing and taking her time to put shave cream next on my beard. (She was so smart. She put the cream on her hands before coming up.) Just about when she was putting a little bit of it on me, I rumbled and did a short snort. I was still *asleep*. She gave out a few short high squeaks a bit running back to her seat, but I was still sleeping.

The next girl, number 3, was coming with her cream lotion on my face and all of a sudden I *woke up*! Whispering in the back and giggling were the gangsters, but there was one more to go as I went back to snoring. Number 4 was the last chance and coming with her lipstick. She put some stripes of red on my face before running back and squeaking all the way. They heard me wake up and told everyone to be quiet because now most of the kids were awake, but all didn't know what happened.

I started feeling stuff all over me, and *realizing* what had happened, I jumped out of my seat and stared at the students in the back and began to *yell!* "Who was doing this? Why in the *world* were you doing this? What for heaven's sake are you thinking?"

"You know, we are just on our way to the East for learning and seeing amazing things. You are not behaving properly that you think such a rude trick like this is…funny?" It became very quiet in the bus quickly.

"Don't you know that whoever has done this could be sent back home to parents and for any unreasonable action, and it can be arranged. Who are the ones responsible?"

A pin would drop, and all would hear. The whole bus was stunned. I just shook my head back and forth and, of course, the girls especially were being very scared of going home, so it was time to change the atmosphere.

"You know, you know what is going to happen, right?" Still quiet. "I am sorry, but I have to tell you and tell you *all!* I and Mrs. Stude planned this whole thing, and I hope you enjoyed the play. It was my *pleasure!*"

It took the bus awhile before they realized it was a trick for sure. Giggles turned into conversation and much laughter, and the girls gave me a hug and others said it was a very cool situation and presentation, and the bus clapped and laughed, and it was just the beginning, dah, dah, dah!

Holocaust Museum

Going to the Holocaust Museum is always a deep, emotional feeling of pain and a disgusting action from human beings being led by demonic powers. Things like this memory of six million plus are an example of such strong spiritual warfare, which has existed ever since this world was created. Hopefully, all gain understanding that Jesus is with us, and he will never leave nor forsake us, and we will be foreknown, predestined, called and just. We all will be glorified!

After studying about the reality of the millions of people involved, many students would go to a prayer room and be touched by the Holy Spirit. The hearts of these teenaged Christians, as well as of this old man Christian, are under God our Father, who was there to meet our needs and strengthen us. When guided by the Word and the Holy Spirit, we are not to be afraid.

The whole practice of genocide has been going on forever, and we keep coming closer and closer to the time we are all in heaven. Understanding Nazi's murdering targeted children? Is it not much different than a Putin or any other non-believing *leader*? Pray for the Power of Jesus! Even my ninety-four-year-old mom is waking in the morning and looking to the sun to see if it might be the day! It is coming.

The kids that went through it all in the museum, each eighth-grader, was paying close attention to what they saw and heard, for all should have learned a great deal more of what WWII was and about the world following the war. Concentration camps and killer centers camouflaged as a nice place, understanding that not only the Jewish people were destroyed, but any race the Nazis would destroy could and would be put away and were considered unequal. Even German

---

people who were people with special needs and/or physically different would/could be destroyed for the Nazi group wanted perfection. It was an awful but spiritual experience for our students and should discuss with parents if needed. Not many kids get such a prize as the East Coast History experience.

It is a rule for teachers, and any chaperones, to do multiple counts to make sure all are there, ending with a count again as they get on the bus. At the end of one trip, we were going to the Ford's Theater where Lincoln was shot by John Wilkes Booth. Just being able to be in such an historical place and the atmosphere makes the history alive!

When we came to a check point, we realized that we were minus one, and soon we were calling up the Holocaust Museum for our student and then talked to Mr. Neis right away to pick him up in the bus. We have solid guides to have all kids at every bus move, and if one is missing, they all have information of what to do if you are "left behind," and it worked out perfectly. The only time it ever happened was when I was on my fourth or fifth trip. Jacob was actually ready to go but quickly walked to get a certain book at the bookshop, and we were gone when he came back out. He also got back in time to see most everything Lincoln.

Andrew

Another cool thing to do, especially on a nice day, is to stand outside the White House to watch from behind the high protected fence that also has unseen protectors, visible police close by for any negative behavior/action and protection on top of the White House with M60 machine guns keeping eyes on the front of all sides.

We could also often be able to view three helicopters coming or going and know that one would be the president, and it was President Obama at this time (my favorite). The two other helicopters were protection as to where the president would be. I always thought that there would sometimes be three false helicopters to be more protective because perhaps it could be possible to shoot down all three?

So it was one of those warm, but not hot, sunny days, with a beautiful blue sky, and there were people showing signs they were against something about changing taxes. It was a common thing to show up, and some people would be in an open wooded place back a little trying to speak on their feelings.

Andrew McFarland was a smart great student, and he loved history. He right away walked up close to the fence to get a good look around the grounds. He was thrilled with what was going on, especially on the roof. He actually got a protected military guy to wave back at him. What happened next was him feeling a couple friends messing with him, and he didn't want to be disturbed. It happened two or three times. What happened next was he felt that tap behind his back, and he was so disturbed and frustrated he quickly turned around to push the boys away. Poor good kid gave a push to a policeman guard. A second guard came up to Andrew to talk with him doing the wrong thing. I had caught sight of this and walked quickly to help let the policeman understand what had happened to the fearful kid and what he was going through. He was scared, he could be in trouble, but the coppers understood I was trying to watch while his *friends* were messing with him, and they both told Andrew they were sorry. Thanks to the guards they understood, and they both explained why they came and said they were glad he was a good kid. I am sure Andrew will never forget this. I know I won't!

Luke

When we went off on this trip, it was when construction was going on all around. The WTC was completed with the Memorial Plaza and twin reflection pools with softly running water. Etched in bronze around the edges of the pools were all the names of those who died. There was a famous restaurant where we would always go for lunch, but at this time, they were only open to all the workers in all the area for free. We were able to go to a couple buildings where we were given an explanation of how everything was going and about the many people lost and the firefighters' strong work. We also learned of what had happened outside of this part of the city on 9/11, namely the destruction of buildings and thousands of people without a choice and the murderous attack on the Pentagon. No one had ever planned for the deliberate attack by a plane loaded with nine thousand gallons of highly inflammable aviation fuel at the World Trade Center.

Luke Larkin had just recently lost his older brother in a sad fashion and losing a brother is an extremely hard core and a long lasting experience to carry. I have a similar experience without losing life. My brother Barry was my hero and we were very close. But after multiple negative things happening in his life, his strong fighting turned into a falling away from our large family. He now is rarely willing to talk anymore, not because of us but because he doesn't feel worthy. Pray for him please, for him to seek out Jesus and be protected from the evil ones.

We took Luke's dad along as a chaperone, especially to be close to Luke. I talked with dad about keeping Luke away from all the death and destruction the rest were going through, and I thought it might be a better break and time to walk a bit away, and dad agreed. Luke and I started walking around some streets when we came to the beautiful music coming from the Saint Paul's Chapel, constructed in 1766, the oldest church building in Manhattan. Located less than one hundred yards from the World Trade Center site, the church became known as "The Little Chapel That Stood" after it survived the collapse of the Twin Towers on 9/11. It is widely believed the church was protected by a giant sycamore tree that was planted in Saint Paul's graveyard.

After just walking around the church for a while, we had to go in and listen. It was a small string ensemble. It was so spiritual that we both had to silently close our eyes and just soak in it while feeling Jesus, and we talked a bit, and we prayed together. We both felt the presence of Jesus with his light in our hearts. A very strong connection! We'll never forget it.

We slowly walked out and were going to another street, but my phone rang. Answering, I heard that the rest of the troops were coming our way. Meeting them all, I don't remember where we went next. I was still in the dream from "The Little Chapel that Stood!"

The New Bus

Most of the eight graders loved just riding through the early morning and the whole night. I really didn't. Bus drivers switched every six hours. All trips were pretty much to the same places, but I tried to add a couple new places that would be solid. We started out with Gettysburg. A cool place to see and be in with such a negative part of war but an important part of our history. Walking around the North and South military set up with canons for artillery and specific tactics to dig in or attack in the war and all the memorials all over the land and bulletholes in houses and an indoor moving map of the war as well as video and memorabilia of the civil war battle.

This group was also able to go out with a northern sergeant who had the kids marching around the grounds, shouting out, and being in a basic military boot camp for fun. The sergeant also gave the opportunity to be sent as a group to where Lincoln gave his famous master speech. The feeling inside of almost hearing Abe in his black coat and top hat—goosebumps for me.

Now another place we went that was the coolest one was going to New York City and seeing the "Naked Cowboy" who is always walking around Broadway, but Broadway is now pedestrian-only, so look for him on Broadway between Forty-Fourth and Forty-Fifth Streets. This is the best place to look first. Kidding, but kids did get a kick. Looking at the corner street sellers had some good deals but be careful. Boys liked to go through expensive sports memorabilia while most girls went for fancy clothes. Going to the One World Observatory or Empire Building are cool on clear days to see the whole city. Last would be getting a fancy supper and a night at a Broadway Theatre while all dressed up in best clothes and make-up.

But wait a minute, just a minute…or maybe hours. Our new bus with cool air had broken down completely. The air-conditioning in the high 90s was no good. We became stuck in a nasty backup and a pretty much inactive, motionless, static, still. We were stuck for about two hours in the tunnel, and it had to be over 100 degrees. No one was sure what was going on, but it was just New York! Luckily we had plenty of water for all, warm water. Students were sweating a lot and started taking off their fancy clothes, but not too much. I was starting to go through heat exhaustion and struggling with my breathing until we finally started moving toward and out of the tunnel. We opened windows even though it was hot, but the air was much better than the tunnel.

Unfortunately, we were possibly going to lose our dinner at Bubba Gump where they are loud and playing games with questions of the Forrest Gump movie and good food. Asking on the phone if they would have a spot for us we got *lucky* and ate fast. So when we finally got out of the bus, properly dressed, it felt like it was spring. With quickly pretty much running, we made it in our fancy clothes, to plop in our soft seats in cool air and were ready for the play *Spider Man*. There were multiple people as Spider Man because he would be flying all over the theatre, and we had one of them right by us as he jumped off the balcony with enjoyment for the kids and teachers. Afterward, we slowly all went back across the Hudson to our hotel without getting stuck in the Lincoln Tunnel and totally tired out.

The last day we got a little extra sleep, packed up all our stuff, and were on our way to the Liberty Statue across the Hudson again. The driver dropped us off and was bringing the bus to hopefully fix things. The ferry gave us a nice ride and dropped us off on the island. We couldn't go up this time as there was construction going on inside the old lady. But we got to walk around and stopped at some stores and chilled until we looked up in the sky. What do we see…The US Army Parachute Team, more widely known as the Golden Knights? They perform around the world as an elite unit and put up a very sweet drop around a specific circle one by one perfectly.

We also stopped out at Ellis Island to learn a little bit of how the thousands and thousands were pouring in to be a part of our country especially after WW I and WW II days. Each ship's manifest log, initially filled out at the ship's port of departure, contained the immigrant's name and answers to twenty-nine questions. This document was used by the legal inspectors at Ellis Island to cross-examine during the legal inspection. They also had to be physically well. Some did have to be quarantined and even sent back. I was able to find the name of Grandpa Swanson but did not have time for Harry Swanson or Grandma Wenberg.

Taking the crowded ferry back to shore, I noticed a man acting strangely. As we all were looking for a seat upper or lower, I kept an eye on the guy with a duffle bag. He found a seat, looked around, put his duffle bag down, and walked away. I didn't see him again. Before we got lined up to get off the ferry, I contacted a couple policemen and just explained what I saw. By the time I got off looking to collect my students, I also saw the police around the same man I told them about. I don't know exactly what the problem was, but I felt like a successful detective.

The kids had some time while waiting for the bus by walking around the ground where there were multiple people selling their goods. Some were okay, and some were illegal but still working or taking off if a policeman was coming. So kids still had fun buying things like fancy fake purses, watches, and other things like hats and colorful scarfs and trinkets.

Well, I had someone to stay in touch about the bus to find out if they had received the newly made part, but it was so new it could only be gotten from Wisconsin and would not be ready. We now were stuck too far to walk with forty-five to fifty kids multiple miles, and we couldn't get a ride but by hitting a close subway. A new adventure!

When we were all to the subway, we had to have cash money or regular tickets but no credit cards. Well, for some reason, we didn't have anything like that to pay for the whole group. Eventually, a very nice lady listened to our problem, and she whispered that we should just go on as a school group, whose bus was unable to help pick us up. I gave her a big hug and a praise of God, for he is good and may God bless that woman!

Then we had to quickly separate our students with chaperones, and we would meet again when we arrived as there might not be enough room for all of us on the first ride in the middle of the afternoon in New York City. Thank you, Jesus! We all made it and created a wonderful memory for us all!

Meeting at the subway, we were to meet the bus and start our hot bus ride home. Since it was going to be hot, the driver set us up to meet another bus with air-conditioning. Changing buses at 2:00 a.m. in east Ohio was not expected. We thought it would be a short ride to change. Collecting all our bags and suitcases and checking that nothing personal was left, the driver said if anything was left he would call the school and send any things he would find.

So back on a cool bus with air-conditioning and *total* exhaustion for all of us, sleep came quickly. Next thing I knew we were pulling into a breakfast restaurant and happy to go in and have a great meal before setting to home. I am sure I gave big hugs to my wife and children and was tired/warn out but glad to get home sweet home and my own bed and family!

Unique Little Things

It was a rule eventually that all cell phones would be kept in bags for girls and for boys by a teacher or two. They would usually only use on the bus to call parents and share with them for a while and put cells back in the bag. Late one night, a couple of boys did not have a cell phone, and Ben Spaulding was kind enough, and he shared his new phone with two other boys. I asked Ken Norman to pick up the last of the boys' cells because they needed a little more time, so Ken collected them and set them next to the girls' phone bag that I had collected.

We were on our way home and tired as usual, and when we got back to CHA, all suitcases and personal material was to be gathered off the bus, to clean out everything, and check the seats to be sure nothing was left and anything that was left would be brought into the school. As cell phones were handed back to the kids, Ben did not get his, and we went through the bus again through every seat and part of the bus with no luck. It was an expensive phone. Mom didn't put up a beef about it, but we started going through the onboard bags/backpacks from the three that used it, and it still didn't show. Dad was not happy. I told Debbie that I would take the blame and pay for the phone since I was in charge. Even though it really wasn't my fault. Debbie from school said the school would cover for it. Never will I ever know where it ended up. The bus driver? No.

Lexi and Brianna were stuck together wherever we went. Were they a bit wacky? Without a doubt. But they could be funny to watch and listen to their talking and talking...It would be very nice and warm during mid-May out East as well as on the bus but Lexi was always wearing a winter-like coat?? It must have been new was my guess. She continued to wear it through most of the places we went. On our way home this time, she realized, after going about one hundred miles closer to home, she must have left her coat at the restaurant for breakfast.

"Stop! We gotta go back to get my coat!" She started to tear a little. "It was a present for me and expensive. We gotta go back!"

Well, we didn't go back, but we did call the restaurant, and they found the coat Lexi described exactly. So her mom was told the story, and we were going to pay the money for shipping the coat to school, but Lexi's mom actually paid for the funky coat by mail, and it was a happy ending for us all.

Red, by the way, when in class one day, she was frustrated and full of anxiety to call for something from home she needed in school. I allowed her to call in class, and she dialed the first three numbers and was frustrated again and hung it up. A little later, not much, a police car came and pulled in by our school's front door. They ran into the school to see what the situation was going on and one officer asked, "Did anyone in the school dial the 911?"

No one in the office knew anything about it, and so it was called throughout the school to hear, "Did anyone dial the 911 phone call?"

Brianna then went super Red and totally embarrassed and replied, "I was trying to call my home but by accident drilled 911 first! I am very sorry!" Red by the way was one who on chapel days wore her skirt up high and was sure to pull it down for chapel. What a stinker.

We had two students that could not make it to go to our East Coast Trips. What we ended up doing was creative as we made a life-like face of each person and connected them to a wood pad for keeping it strong so we could take pictures of the many places we were and put their faces right into the groups. It was a way to keep in touch and hopefully give a couple kids some way of being with us. We brought some things back to give to them also. Lukas T. had a broken arm or leg. I don't remember thirteen years later the name of the student who had a severe peanut allergy and would have a dangerous reaction to anything with peanut in it. So mom was wise to not take any chances with all the different restaurants and without mom being able to come along they just couldn't send him.

On the trip that Carter Coughlin was on, everywhere we went, he was followed by girls from a different group. Especially when we were in all the different museums in DC, he could be surrounded by girls from other schools. Poor guy. Not!

Noah Woods was one of my favorite kids who got me in trouble with his dad until he understood what was happening. One class person created a project after the trip and built his own pillory where people would be seen with their hands and head stuck in it. Often people would spend a short time in the pillory several hours before being imprisoned. Well, everyone in class wanted to try it out, and Noah not only wanted to put himself in it but also wanted to spend half the class doing his work that way. Well, he told mom about it, and dad took it the wrong way, and he, after a talk with me, understood it was not a negative. Noah said by going all over historical places he learned more than he ever thought. He learned much, and I got a great feeling to hear about that.

Many students on one trip got to meet Senator Bob Dole at the WWII memorial during a lucky day where many WWII warriors would be flown to DC and meet old-timers and the Memorials and all our students were asked to talk to at least one soldier and thank them for their service. Some of us got a close hello to Bob Dole and got pictures with him.

One other thing is when I was watching the night until the hotel security came, I caught Micaela Pekarek peeking out the door with a smile and started to walk out when she saw me and giggled and jumped back in their room. I heard that the room tried to come out later but ran right back in but was sent back in by a protector who was there all night. Cute.

Final Test in Eighth-Grade History

The last test in eighth grade is while on the bus ride between all the wonderful historical places just fly by constantly. So do your best to get the best and use a diary form to put thoughts from previous neoclassical monuments and buildings and unique museums and historical ground and more. It can be a once-in-a-lifetime experience.

Find a little time when you are able to write down how the sites struck your ideas or thoughts and things you never knew that were fantastic and why it was so cool. Also, the Holocaust should remain in your brain while it struggles to accept the evil in our world.

Be sure to take as many pictures as you can. Fun pictures of your fellow students are fine as are bus pictures, but be sure to try and get as many pics from each super site and eventually put a short headline under the pic. Washington is full of history, and museums are full even more. Make your choices. Memorials like WWI and WWII, Iwo Jima Statue and the Arlington National Cemetery with thousands and thousands of soldiers who fought for our country.

Arlington House, The Robert E. Lee Memorial

The Unknown Soldier and the changing of the guard is more than worthwhile, taking it in and remembering the site. Write down the stories of these special men and what they have to go through, having to be perfect in everything they do. Since April 6, 1948, this tomb has been guarded twenty-four hours a day, 365 days a year, with zero exception. Each guard has to be in superb physical condition and have an unblemished military record, and they receive no extra pay. They agree to not disgrace the uniform in any way, including not swearing or drinking alcohol on or off duty or for the rest of their lives. Include for sure New York City and just walking around and seeing a Broadway Play and the fun you have with your friends. Good streets have sellers on most every corner and some of the hats and shirts and jackets and small things showing the city can be bought.

Gettysburg, Washington's Farm, Jefferson's uncommon house can all be looked back at years from now by this *last eighth grade test*. Be sure all the time you spent is great to put in your photo book with text. These things will get you an A+++. Don't forget any little things like tickets, brochures, and any piece of the trip that makes sense in your book.

Minnesota New Country School

Located in Henderson, Minnesota, MNCS Elementary opened its doors to students for the first time on August 26, 2013. The elementary had eighty-five students enrolled in kindergarten through sixth grade from thirteen surrounding communities within a forty-five-mile radius.

As a tuition-free public charter school, MNCS receives state funding and provides bus transportation to the communities it serves.

MNCS Elementary follows a project-based curriculum where students each receive an individualized learning plan. While there is still a focus on basic skills such as math, reading and writing, MNCS teachers also focus heavily on (1) environmental experiential learning; (2) project-based learning; (3) responsive classroom; (4) character education; and (5) technology.

When I first started, I was introduced to the head of the elementary ancient building. It had been refurbished inside but still a castle outside. I was hired right away after Christmas. Jenny was a super Christian, and she took me around the building after the long interview. Our talk certainly showed how we both were for Jesus. Her husband was a Christian also. Chris was finishing his bachelor degree, and they both worked with young teens at their church. They both went on a month-long mission that first summer as their *honeymoon*. That is how dedicated they were. On the next year, Jenna was pregnant and to have a baby in the spring. The staff was collecting money to get them a nice present before the summer, but I decided to get this antique, well-built, wooden, Noah's Ark baby rocker. Unfortunately, for me, they were leaving after their second year and moved on to bring Jesus to others as they were surely of God.

The K-12 grades were unique to say the least. Many students had come from their local school, and some were not treated well before coming to MNCS. Luckily, there were some elementary Christian believers. Another unique Christian was Abraham who was an older married man about twenty-five, and I was talking Jesus with him at times with a pleasure and a positive example for non-Christians in the school that might help. Abe would always be eating a homemade hot, delicious-looking and -smelling lunch. One day I said to him, "Your wife must be a great cook for all the lunches she makes for you!" He then answered, "Oh, she is the best, especially her soups, meat pie, and beef stew. Maybe I'll have her send some lunch for you."

Well, two days later, he came into my room with a hot bowl of beef stew that *was* super, mucho tasty! I wrote a thankful note for him to bring home, and she got a kick out of it. Soon his eight weeks were over, and even though everyone wanted him to stay, he was planning for years he would be working in his plantation where all people stuck together and continued working the farms but also teaching children. Hutterites are strong with biblical doctrine and Christians believing in adult baptism and pacifism, as do other Anabaptists such as the Mennonites, the Amish, and the Brethren in Christ, yet they also follow biblical texts enjoining strict community of goods.

There were a few other Christians with us however. One was a music/PE teacher whose nickname was Sunshine, and I was Moon Beam. Another was the first- or second-grade teacher who was a dedicated reading teacher as she was dyslexic herself, and we worked together often in the reading area especially. Our nurse was a very nice believer also and shared a crowded room; we both got through it and got to be good friends as well as the para/kitchen lady who turned out to be at the same Sedalia, Missouri Rock Week from many years ago, and it was a surprise to me!

Before being hired by MNCS, since I was so rudely let go from Chapel Hill, I was struggling for sure. To be fifty-nine years old, not many would be up for taking me because of the amount of money needed for someone old and with lots of teaching. There were not going to be many people trying to hire me. The longer you teach, the more money you make, and that was not probable for my hope.

I was actually planning to work at the Chapel Hill school for two more years so I could have Elijah for his last two years. I was offered that Eli could stay in the school still, but it didn't work out well, and they complained about him staying too late because Karen worked until five thirty. No more singing in the car every day I took my kids to school. No more reading Scripture on the way to school or back to the house.

I did quite a bit subbing for a few specific schools into the fall. A couple schools in Rockford, Minnesota, went well working with small groups of struggling students and filling in for multiple classes. It started to help me feel a little better.

Cologne was a great place for me as I worked quite a bit with special needs students, full classes from first grade to eighth graders. I received nothing but great esteem as a part of the group and asked to be at meetings with the rest of the staff. I even stepped in for the music class with good help of what I would do with the kids. Two of the kids were from church, and parents were the helpers. Anyway, as much as I had a pretty consistent fill-in job here, I came to an opportunity for a project-based elementary school called MNCS. Site-based teams (operations and management) such as: Art and Literature, Health & Wellness, Nutrition & Compost, PBL, Finance, Personnel, Career/Future/Tech Ed, Supporting Students Together, Outreach, Transportation, Building, Academic Assessment, Q-Comp, Math, Reading, HS/Elem Connections, along with sophomore, junior, and senior teams. So you can see that we had more to do then our personal teaching. We worked together going into at least three of the above jobs. We were the clan of principal and superintendent!

My initial preview with about ten staff, I did very well and really liked the situation. This is a school that is controlled by everyone who is teaching and helping each other. When I first started full time, I was introduced to the head of the new elementary in early January.

I remember my first Christmas at MNCS when, like many schools, would have staff pick a card from a hat for the person you would buy a present at a modest amount of money. Jenna picked

Aaron who came with experience from the high school and was very athletic in all major sports. He also, for some reason—I never found out completely why—he stayed away from church-related information. He was seemingly against anything to do with Jesus. Perhaps it was more for whatever church he was once a member. Although, a couple of us heard the church bells in town and just ringing hymns and Aaron knew most of the words.

Something must have happened to destroy his faith, which is just what Satan and his army are out to do! I still pray for his salvation as well as for other people at that school. By the way, Jenna gave Aaron a present of wooden angels for his gift. He gave it back to her, and she kept finding other places that would be his. One last try was putting it in his mailbox. He denied. So Jenna gave it to me, and I hung it on my wall…just where he could see it. Those angels of protection are still on our front door of our house. Oh, and there was a 7'1" long blond-haired dude who loved to work with kids, especially with nature that he knows very well. Christopher was an avid, dedicated atheist with constant opposite views when I brought up Jesus. He is one I pray for his salvation too as well as all the many beautiful kids I had the blessing to be with.

I was struggling at first, and I started taking workshops at least two or three times the first year. I had to try out multiple educational services to see what was good for who in learning. I enjoyed the work it took to build a strong curriculum until I went through the long class of Orton Gillingham's process that has been around for a long time and was supergood for the kids. I built in reading daily and eventually every other day because more kids needed help. I must say that we all had opportunity to go to multiple workshops every year.

Many kids were tested and shown to be dyslexic in various ways but mostly the struggle to read. The sequence of letters and symbols like numbers would be confusing. Some would be easily distracted so one-on-one teaching would help to focus. The start is understanding the sounds each letter could make and drill it every day possible until they nail it. After the individual letters are letters together and I used cards, hands-on games, and online pictures to drill with until the section of blended letters is successful. There are many more

pieces to strengthening reading with short words, hit, pit, wit, lit…
and building to syllabication. Also using multisensory grammar to
actually *overlearn* concepts.

All children had projects to work on as well as reading, math,
history, music and science with many related ways to learn by taking
trips. We would go to the Ney Nature Center just up the road across
the Minnesota River. Nature workers would give talks and use animals and plants and safety to learn. We would also go out in small
groups to build protection in cold weather and build from nature.
Going to the ponds to check the water and any animals nearby. We
would be out in the woods to find the Maple trees and slowly get
the sap out in the Spring and turn the buckets until all trees were
completed. It would be cooked into syrup, and the kids would sell
some of it and there would always be a day to have all cooking up
pancakes. All done by the kids.

Hunting in nearby woods a fun project was looking for the
mushrooms in the spring. The morel mushroom (also called yellow
morels or sponge mushrooms) is known around the world but is
most prevalent in the northern hemisphere. Morel mushrooms are
probably the most recognizable and sought-after edible mushroom.
Morels usually emerge annually in the spring when there has been
adequate rainfall. In southern Minnesota, they can be found in late
April through May, depending on the rainfall and temperature.
Northern Minnesota may see morels into June.

A little ways from the schools, groups of students would be
going up a steep hill to end in flat land where kids would be working
on the fifteen different kinds of apple trees, checking the bee hives
and working on the large garden and cleaning the area if needed.
A large fence was built years ago by older students that was about
ten feet high to protect any *stealing* from the deer. In the fall, every
student would have days to go up and start collecting the apples and
getting rid of the no-good apples, and these would eventually turn
the apples into juice and be sold and save some for hot cider in the
winter and sell the apples as they were. Same with the bee hives.

From bee

Honey starts as flower nectar collected by bees, which gets broken down into simple sugars stored inside the honeycomb. The design of the honeycomb and constant fanning of the bees' wings causes evaporation, creating sweet liquid honey. Honey's color and flavor vary based on the nectar collected by the bees. For example, honey made from orange blossom nectar might be light in color, whereas honey from avocado or wildflowers might have a dark amber color.

To hive

On average, a hive will produce about 55 pounds of surplus honey each year. Beekeepers harvest it by collecting the honeycomb frames and scraping off the wax cap that bees make to seal off honey in each cell. Once the caps are removed, the frames are placed in an extractor, a centrifuge that spins the frames, forcing honey out of the comb.

To home

After the honey is extracted, it's strained to remove any remaining wax and other particles. Some beekeepers and bottlers might heat the honey to make this process easier, but that doesn't alter the liquid's natural composition.

After straining, it's time to bottle, label, and bring it to you. It doesn't matter if the container is glass or plastic, or if the honey is purchased at the grocery store or farmers' market. If the ingredient label says "pure honey," nothing was added from bee to hive to bottle. Project Learning!

When the garden food was taken care of all summer on their own time, the potatoes, corn, squash, lettuce, cabbage, green beans, and other food would be used to sell at the farmers' market and use the money to help people in need.

Great egrets, great blue herons and nesting waterfowl such as mallards, hooded mergansers, wood ducks, and Canada geese are rearing their young in and around wetlands, and the Minnesota River. The white and young eagles can be seen all over, and especially in the spring and fall, they can be found in *huge* amounts of togetherness, which is an amazing view and sounds.

The Minnesota River is unhealthy. Sediment clouds the water, phosphorus causes algae, nitrogen poses risks to humans and fish, and bacteria make the water unsafe for swimming. Too much water flowing into the river plays a big part in all these problems. These are all projects students can use to understand what is wrong and how they might help to clean. Canoeing is a project the older kids do many times each year…at least.

There are some parents that have a farm and kids would come in groups to work with the earth and helping growing food and weeding and watering and picking food as above to get the experience of being a farmer. There would also be multiple different animals that kids could work with in feeding and cleaning the poop and brushing horses down while some could work with the baby and young pigs. We always would go to the Minnesota Zoo and the cool Reptile and Amphibian Discovery Zoo in Medford.

School plays and musicals written especially for kids to perform

Hopkins is another theatre we went to as the whole K-6 kids would be there. Stages Theatre Company is committed to addressing barriers that can restrict participation to our performances and programming. We believe that every individual should be able to access the joy, wonder, and benefits of participation in the theatre arts. We are working toward a future beyond compliance, toward a fully inclusive environment where all programs and performances are accessible to all.

Adapted for Young Performers: Speeches are short, and dialogue and vocabulary are appropriate for child performers ages six to twelve or older.

Flexible casts of around twenty-five to thirty-five students doubling roles and adding extras possible for smaller or larger casts. Every role has a name and at least three spoken lines or significant action or movement. Large parts are divided so that no one child becomes the *star* or has to memorize too many lines. Line counts and transitions are shown in the scripts. About forty to forty-five minutes long. The plays are long enough to be substantial presentations and short enough to accommodate your teaching schedule and easy costumes and scenery; we provide many suggestions on how to create or find what you need to make a great-looking production without breaking your budget. Every kid in the school would be a part of the play and groups would have songs related to the play. Kids and parents and we teachers loved the whole process coming through as a super presentation! It was always downtown at the Raud House.

We would also hit Museums like Children's Museum in St. Paul, Children's Museum of Southern Minnesota, Mankato, Minnesota, and Art museums and Native American museums and Minnesota Symphony and Orchestra.

All those seventeen site-based teams would all get together usually sometime in May and work as our specific teams and as a whole team. Preparing for the summer ideas and the next year's needs was used at work for sure. *However*, most would all join in vans from Henderson but I would drive myself after a couple of years because it was hours of driving to MNCS and the Lanesboro area. Home of many Amish farmers. Getting to our cabins, that are very well set up as you can get the idea. The boys would sleep in one and another cabin for the girls that was just as beautiful inside. Fireplaces and nice kitchens and most beds okay.

When everyone started getting there we would get our bedrooms and beds, put away our *stuff*, and help to bring in the food to the girls' cabin. After all is ready we would have a small group that would set up lunch for us all. Breakfast, lunch, and supper were for different groups to set everything up food-wise and clean up after. Different groups would take turns doing all that.

After lunch, we would have an all-staff discussion and then break into our specific groups to begin what to get done these three days and set up days in the summer to meet at school. There would be all kinds of candy and always the *big* see-through bowl with the orange, round, crunchy Cheetos. There would also be various veggies. Supper would come, and we would have more meetings trying to get as much as possible done that first day. There would be time for some to play volleyball, but I would just watch for a while and go in with some others to watch the NBA games going for any games in the finals.

The second day would be working after a short discussion and/ or some get-to-know-each-other *stuff*. Continue work, have lunch and usually take a break for staff's choice. Canoeing on the Root River is cool. I only did it once, but it was a time when our *more than a secretary* was rowing with two others and fell in through some rapids and then was stuck in a tiny patch of mud in the middle of the rapids.

We got people from the cabin to help get us in line with rope to help her as a group to pull her to safety. She did lose her shoes. She also took it like a tough shot. There were also bikes we were allowed to use and on a trail, or we could just take a nice walk or do a little fishing. Usually in the bright evening, there would be some weird setup for small groups (three to four) to try and outscore others with Frisbee golf, beanbag corn hole game, ladder toss, croquet game, and many other weird found setups. Most loved to play volleyball as the evening got dark. It was a good way to get to know some better and a time to relax and a break from school.

Heaven Would Be a Better Place
Karen's Perspective

"Heaven would be a better place for anyone." Saturday morning, I took Doug down to 212 Urgent Care in Chaska, and he was holding my arm as we walked in. That was the first clue to the seriousness of the illness. While we were there, they had him change into a gown and hook him to some fluids. He became increasingly somnolent. (I learned that word that very day.) While we were there, they said he should be transferred to Waconia because he should at least stay overnight to get fluids.

The doctor came back after about half an hour later and said he needed to go to either Abbott Hospital or North Memorial in case he needed dialysis for his kidneys. "That was the second clue to the seriousness of his illness" (but not really because they did say "in case"). I asked the nurse, "On a scale of 1–10, is it serious?" She answered, "Well, he is really pretty sick."

I remember feeling frustrated with that answer at that time, but if she had said "nine or ten," could I have been able to handle that? I don't know. We had picked Abbott, but the doctor said there were no ICU beds available, nor was North Memorial available! So he was sent to the teaching hospital of HCMC in Minneapolis. That was the third clue to the seriousness.

So we waited for them to bring the ambulance for Doug. They took him with his IV, and I took his clothes. I could have ridden with him, but I thought it made more sense to bring the car over there so we weren't stranded when we left the next day. I had been praying all morning in the ER and in the car. Of course, it had to be tricky to get to HCMC on a Saturday because a lot of it was blocked off, and I actually parked in the wrong ramp.

When I got there, Doug said he had to pee and he was given a handheld urinal. He asked me to guard the curtain on the tiny ER room, and he tried in his open cloth but couldn't go at all. He wanted to go down to the bathroom but was too tired. He laid down instead.

Then someone came in and said he was going to the STAB (pronounced STAYB) Room, which I assumed meant "stabilizing room." (This was when they must have gotten his counts back.)

Another person came to talk to me, and I remember asking questions about him when there seemed there was a problem protecting his airway. I'm still not clear about that. I asked other questions but can't remember what they were. At this point, I was still praying of course, but I think I was in some level of shock.

Someone took me back to the family waiting room just for the ER to wait. In hindsight, they were probably getting me out of the main area of the ER so that it wouldn't be a big scene if they had to tell me he died. That should have been the fifth clue to the seriousness of his illness, and still I wondered when I could see him.

Chaplain Steve came in to talk with me in a private waiting room. (B3, I think.) He got me some orange juice and told me the doctor would be coming to see me soon. That was the sixth clue to the seriousness of Doug's illness. I caught on to that one, and yet I had my doubts because maybe they always have a visit to everyone who comes into the ER. (I knew it wasn't true.)

About forty-five minutes later, Dr. Bob Mettit came in; he is a resident at HCMC. He explained what was going on, and it made sense, but I couldn't have repeated it much. It sounded like it could be a life-or-death situation, so I posed that question to him. He said yes. Thank you! No sugarcoating or nice words. I also asked if I should call the kids to come. He said yes. That was the seventh clue...no more clues! That was a straightforward answer to my question. He might die.

They left me alone for a while. I was praying, and God had already given me peace during this. It is an amazing and unexplainable faith. For whatever happened, it would be for the good of those who love and serve him. I even got mad at myself for being *okay* with the possibility of Doug dying. But I did reassure myself that Doug would be in a better place, even though he wouldn't want to leave his family.

I felt I "should be" crying hysterically and asking God why and only praying for Doug to get better. Another part of me saw that as selfish. Why would I want God to leave him here if he needed him in heaven? Heaven would be a better place for anyone.

Parts of James 5:15–16: "Pray for each other so that you may be healed. The prayer of a righteous man (or woman) is powerful and effective."

Doug's Perspective

I struggled to get in the car for a ride to Chaska. When I arrived, I slowly walked inside and sat down with a red beach bucket for a puke emergency. Things were about to change drastically. I remember the CAT scan, though, I thought it was at Chaska. I must have been set up with medication in my IV as I was rushed to HCMC by ambulance, but I was not sure what was going on. I was somewhat conscious when arriving because I could smell the exhaust before they rushed my gurney inside. I think I met Bob while they brought me in, and he was first to check out the problem.

CAT scan used to look at kidneys, heart, lungs, and more.

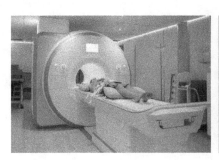

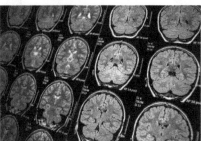

| Cat scan | Used to look at kidneys, heart, lungs and more |

Into the darkness: I remember the CAT scan roughly but I thought it was at Hennepin County Medical Hospital. I must have been getting some type of a sedative in my IV as we left Chaska by ambulance but I was not too sure of anything. I was surprised to find out many days later that Karen didn't even forget my red puke bucket. I was a bit conscious when arriving at HCMC, and I can still smell the exhaust from the garage vehicles coming in and out as I was wheeled inside to begin the war.

More memories had some pretty dark ones. I came to this struggle and going where I didn't know. There was a significant lapse of time with no recall whatsoever. I was present but not really a participant of what seemed like an hour after morbid movies or morbid live performances. What was actually the first long day everything went away, and I started to watch doctors and nurses below me. It wasn't clear, but I could hear people with light-blue clothes and mask talking, but I couldn't hear what they were saying. That was when I faded away and must have eventually started to sleep quietly.

When I *awoke*, I heard sirens going on outside, and I heard nurses talking away from me, but the room was dark, and I was not sure if anyone was taking care of me. I was yelling, though my catheter down my throat would actually not allow it, and I felt I was in trouble, but eventually someone came in and tried to talk me down, but I found out much later I was turning my head hard left and right, and it was capable of messing up the main artery and more. So they must have put in more fentanyl to shut me down.

When I came out of medicinal warfare for days, I came out slowly. Looking at the wall and ceiling with an army of little ants, my family and doctors were watching in the room. I was staring at the multiple buggers continuing to move down to the floor. I asked daughter Annika if she saw what I saw, and she just moved her head left and right. I asked for anyone to tell me why this is happening in a hospital!

Eventually a doctor explained that because of all the *medicine*, I went through hallucinations, and they might hang for a while. Understanding why the ants did not leave made some sense. Earlier when I heard terrible demonic music that made me cry out: "What kind of music is playing in the large room with my family and why can't a person cut it off!" Well, I couldn't have been talking at all as I had been intubated.

The next memories are scattered and dark. I came to the obscurity knowing there was an interruption of some significance with no recall before the coming moments. I was present but not really participant of what seemed like hour after hour of movies or better yet of visions. These visions included many people and many of these people were on the younger side.

They were struggling for sure and some in pain, and many seemed to be South Asian. I tried to sit down before some, and they could not understand me. Young ones with deformity or some physical struggle, and I could not help! I walked among them not feeling necessarily threatened, but curious and even willing to help if it was needed. However, this continued on to the point where I started feeling like this was it. This is where I am right now. I must be dead. This is for real. It is not a place of comfort, joy, or love.

"Jesus!" "What is going on here?" "I know you, Jesus, why are you not here with me?" "Please come and take me away!"

I cried out to him and felt, "Was I a fraud? Is Jesus a fraud?" I was confused and fearful and felt, just to clarify, Satan was taking advantage of my condition and that my brain was filled with propofol and fentanyl.

I think Jesus answered me as I don't remember much more similar to all that. The next *phase* of this dreamlike atmosphere was as I oversaw from above multiple people of a surgical team doing their work. It was too blurry to see much specifically, but I saw something like their silhouettes and gowns at times and moments of moving around a *centerpiece*. They were talking back and forth with instruction-like talk, but again I have no specific words of recall. Boredom came upon me for lack of understanding exactly what was going on.

Next I found myself in a wheelchair (except I was really still tied down in the ICU). I felt like we were in an open family-like room without much light. At first, I could hear family members talking, but I was totally paralyzed to the point where I could not talk or move any part of my body at all. I also could not see anything or anyone, which led to my imagination fueled by the drugs.

Again, it was like a movie projector showing imaginary movies that I thought were real. There was demonic music with demonic lyrics. I wondered why in the world would a hospital allow someone to play this music. Slowly, I was able to start moving my little finger on my right hand. At a snail's pace, I was able to move more fingers. I remember futilely trying to figure out what was in my mouth. People were trying to calm me down and guess my thoughts as I could not communicate in any way. It frustrated me terribly which is why I was able to swing my head back and forth to get rid of this obstruction (which was my catheter for oxygen). Finally, there was a little time of being settled down a bit as Karen said while holding my hand, "I love you!" I was able to lightly squeeze her hand four times to send my love *too* back to her. I did something similar to my eighty-eight-year-old mother.

I eventually heard my kids talking and other family talking until it came time for them all to leave. Some back home, some with Nancy, and one to Grandma's house.

The Saturday after my release I was made to realize that I was in the ICU for four days with all the catheters, ventilator, dialysis machine, and multiple IVs. I had been under the impression it only lasted Saturday to Sunday. Thus, the photos with my kids were over those days when they were around. When I was somewhat clearer minded, without as much hallucination, I struggled with time as I missed most of the four days. It was Tuesday, not Sunday.

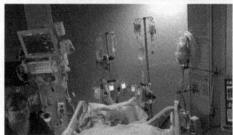

Nothing But the Blood of Jesus

My whole body was being attacked by toxins caused by very severe lactic acidosis, pancreatitis, and the shutting down of my kidneys as a reaction to the poison. My brain was also going through chemical changes because of the above as well as multiple medications. Add that my body was in septic shock, delirious, and there is no question that my blood needed to be cleansed continually for five days. My thoughts are brought now to the blood of Jesus. He is the dialysis for my very soul. Father God now sees me through the perfect and sinless blood of Jesus Christ. All who believe are no longer under rule of the law but by faith, and above all grace, I/we are saved.

> God presented Him (Jesus) as a sacrifice of atonement, through faith in His blood. (Romans 3:25a)

> Since we have now been justified by His blood, how much more shall we be saved from God's wrath through Him! (Romans 5:9)

> In Him we have redemption through His blood, the forgiveness of sins in accordance with the riches of God's grace. (Ephesians 1:7)

> The blood of Jesus, His Son, purifies us from all sin. (1 John 1:7b)

Testing came for a variety of things and many on the same day. My worst one was blood being *scraped* out and was painful sometimes, but I don't know why that would be needed. Still don't. Checking all medical tests from my kidneys, of course, my heart and liver and especially what my creatinine was at, which was a close look constantly to check if it was dropping, which would be a good thing.

Being able to go to the bathroom and take off my clothes, sit down, and put them back on wasn't easy but I worked it out. Being able to drink some water without choking and the same with a small cookie. I was fine with that one. There were more exams to be checked to be able to leave.

When those specific medical workers began to allow me to start working physically and mentally and passed, the head doctor approved for me to go to rehabilitation. It was slow multiple sections to strengthen me in many ways physically. Just standing up was a start and as time went, I would be taking steps with bars to hold. After that, I would work with a nurse holding me with a rubber strap for support. I worked my way to walk up and down stairs and walked looking up just to see if I would get woozy.

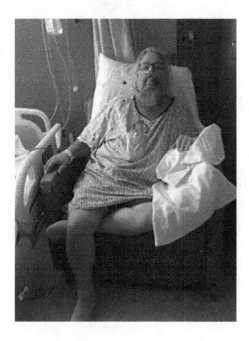

After being in HCMC for two weeks and having family in everyday and my wife sleeping next to me in a crappy *bed* next to mine, I was able to not only get out but was able to rehabilitate at my home for six to eight weeks. I must say that having family in the hospital and watching NFL football was not bad, and my wife was given sandwiches, which were sneaked into my room by the chef so she could eat while I ate my meal. He was impressed by how she was staying by my side continually. Lastly, from the nurses especially, I ended up with the nickname of Dougie Fresh, and it went on to my school. However, one sweet nurse saw my name on the white board and said, "You're not no Dougie Fresh!" It was said in fun. Every doctor and nurse was fantastic! *Thank you, Jesus!*

> For he has rescued us from the dominion of darkness and brought us into the kingdom of the Son he loves, in whom we have redemption, the forgiveness of sins. (Colossians 1:13)

> I love the LORD for he heard my voice; he heard my cry for mercy. Because he turned his head to me, I will call unto him as long as I live. The cords of death entangled me, the anguish of the grave came upon me, and I was overcome with trouble and sorrow. Then I called upon the name of the LORD: OH LORD save me! (Psalm 116:1–3)

Doctor notes from HCMC, ER, and ICU

January 7, 2017, 1:13 p.m.
Brought to STAB room due to abnormal labs of metabolic acidosis
    with altered mental status, acute renal failure, and septic shock
2:12 p.m.
Support spouse (Karen) who arrives and hears medical update regarding severity of prognosis. Karen is contacting family to come.
    Karen affirms Christian faith for her family and prayer is offered
2:27 p.m.

Patient intubated
2:52 p.m.
Very severe lactic acidosis…shock
3:42 p.m.
Adult Medical Resuscitation, airway intubation, artery line and central venous line
3:44 p.m.
Radiologist satisfied with appearance of endotracheal tube
Aspiration/pneumonia cannot be excluded, especially at left lung base
Upon arrival to STAB room, vitals were concerning for hypotension, tachycardia, and tachypnea
Blood pressure remained in 60s
Femoral line was placed after failure of R radial line
Central line to R jugular
9:14 p.m.
Needs emergent dialysis

January 8, 2017, 7:39 a.m.
Wide awake writing notes? Wanted to be extubated
11:23 a.m.
Awakens easily when sedation lightens
Septic shock
Wean down propofol

January 9, 2017
3:32 p.m.
Patient not interactive; spouse, sister-in-law, mother in room; sister and other family in waiting area
6:06 p.m.
Vent weaning, patient calm, able to follow commands
Spontaneous breathing trial stopped for safety
Doug is strong and at risk for self-extubating; also shakes head side-to-side causing pressure on cart

January 10, 2017

7:26 a.m.

Awake, drowsy but attempting to respond to commands

11:10 a.m.

Weaned off fentanyl and propofol, eyes opened spontaneously, intermittently followed commands

Tolerated weaning as extubated. Followed commands, confused

3:46 p.m.

Confused during examination, easily distracted, required redirection to focus on drinking water mush

4:51 p.m.

Able to maintain stable vitals through exercises, able to follow one-step commands, unable to answer pertinent history questions or provide social information

My Last Year at MNCS

It was a struggling six months with the pandemic and the thousands and thousands and millions of people dying all over the world. I was very sad to leave a staff that was dedicated and working harder than any group I had ever been with. I still miss the young children who were worth more than any money and money is not what I wanted. I wanted to work with struggling children and their parents, and it was a gift from God for me. Therefore, the pandemic going strong I retired and didn't know what to do. My whole family was locked in the house for ten days and had COVID breakouts with everyone in our family more than once.

Then I was taking Eli to bring the gerbils to the Andersons' farm about seventy miles from Mayer. I was not feeling well at all after driving for a while. When we got there all the kids came out to meet the new animals. All six of them who brought two kindergartners, two first graders, one in third and one in fourth. I worked with all of them, and they had to be driven thirty-plus miles each day to and from the school.

I was happy to see them all as well as mom and dad, but it was very hot. They showed me around all the different animals outside freely and inside, but I was in need of water, and it wasn't helping much. They showed us egging snakes and a good-size lizard inside, and the little guy adopted from Russia was all over the gerbils, and the gerbils were enjoying him. We also brought food and a cage for the rodents. I let ma and pa know later that I was not well and ended going to the hospital *again* for a few days and testing and came out okay. The next summer, when Eli graduated from high school and Ethan from college, we invited all the Andersons to Grandma's house for a grad party, and it was nice to hang out with them again…healthy.

Papa Howie

Callin' me peanut, callin me chief
Callin' me forgiven, when I played the thief
Popcorn was shuffled, in a soot bottom pan
Sharing with my daddy, buttered love from a man

Midnight pizza from Ledos, a dying grandpa daily met
Why couldn't I follow, the example you set
Through my car wrecks and obstacles, you were always there
How blind could my youth be, to not see how he cared?

Papa, so much has happened since you went away
The Word took root at Moody, and is still alive today
Papa, so much has happened since you went away
I asked a jewel in my life, she said she'd come to stay

Butch and the raccoons, the bed on the porch
No window in the Rambler, hidden fear and remorse
The fightin' with Mama, left bright scars dipped in pain
The wounds have healed over, but the sadness remains

Fish calls on Vermilion, the laughter at night
Are the reasons it's still sacred, to camp on that sight
I see you in me, I am truly your son
A child looked up to you
Now I am the one, I am the won

My father worked almost every day and fifty to sixty hours a week to take care of our large family. Though he had trouble with alcohol during his later days and lost marriage to my mom, he came back to Jesus and died at the age of sixty-four and is in heaven for sure.

Brother Lost and Alone

Where did you go and what did I do?
Why hasn't God paid a visit to you?
Pleadings are set through emotional tools,
Why did you go, and what more can I do?

I know a long love was lost, it is known to be true.
Beguiled by the prince of this sick and lost world
What are you doing know, what can you say?
Why hasn't The Spirit, whispered in your heart and mind?

The lovers who bore you, they scuffled til they lost.
We as the seedlings, paid a thorn painful cost.
More me than the others and more you than me.
How long will you be blinded by a pierced mystery being?

Have you been baited, persuaded by shachath?
Could you be buried with none to know your death?
Are there deeper meanings with feelings in the way?
Will I meet you in heaven through grace and sound faith?

Shepherd come to feed us, be a blaze to lead through the night.
Burn away our deceivers and the hardness inside.
In the name of Messiah who sacrificed his life.
Be free from your torment and be blessed into the *light*.

Brother Barry was very high in grades, sports, church and loved by everyone. After college, he was to get married to a beautiful woman, but multiple things happened quickly. He was very close to Grandma Swanson as she was close to him in keeping his faith strong. She passed away the same time as my parents divorced, and Grandpa Swanson passed away too. He got to the point that he would not be the one for his wife-to-be. That ended up in his best friend marrying his loved one. There was more to it than that, but he became a loner and would spend much time with his writing and music and would be in the country of beautiful Sweden every other year. I pray for him often and ask Jesus if I will meet him up north some day when everything is without pain and fear but with joy forever and the face of Jesus Christ. I haven't seen him since thirty years ago when we took him to a Twins game. I still love him and pray for him constantly. You could be great to pray too.

"I Can See the Lord in My Life"

```
      Am                          Dm
V1  It came upon the day when I could finally say,
      G                                    C
    "I no longer live according to the world's ways."
      F                            Dm
    A time when all my sin, to God, would be erased
      E                          Am
    By the pain-stained wood below my loving Savior's face.
      Am                          Dm
V2  By faith, a gift from God, we're reckoned righteous in His eyes,
      G                                    C
    All because a humble servant took our cross and died…
      F                        Dm
    Foreknown, predestined, called, and just, we all shall be glorified.
      E                                    Am
    First fruits, the Holy Spirit, given proof to be our guide.
```

```
Refrain
      Dm
    I can see the Lord in my life.
      G             C
    I believe in the Lord in my life.
```

F   Dm
Though I long tried to hide from His sight,
E   Am
I can now see my Lord.
Am   Dm

V3 He saved me from a life of everlasting gloom.
  G   C
  Such love, grace, and direction, I never knew.
  F   Dm
  I thank you, Lord and Savior, for letting me be in You.
  E   Am
  I hope I understand just what you want me to do.